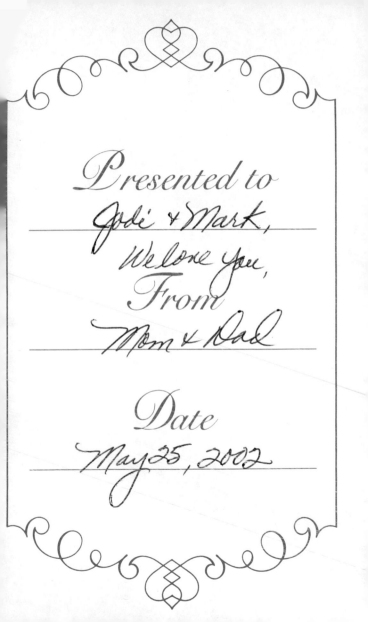

Presented to

Jodi & Mark,

We love you,

From

Mom & Dad

Date

May 25, 2002

I am my beloved's and my beloved is mine...
SONG OF SOLOMON 6:3

Unless otherwise noted Scripture quotations are from
The Holy Bible, King James Version.

Library of Congress Cataloging-in-Publication Data

Forever in love.
    p.   cm.
  ISBN 0-8499-51534
  1. Married people—Prayer-books and devotions—
English.   2. Love—Religious aspects—Christianity—
Prayer-books and devotions—English.   I. Word
Publishing.
BV4596.M3F67   1995
242'.644—dc20

                                        95-18138
                                           CIP

                ISBN 0-8499-5153-4

            Printed in Belgium

$\mathcal{C}$ontents

Learning to Love

*A*ll of the gold and silver in the world is not worth as much as the abiding true love of another. Give your love as a precious gift to a mate worthy of your care and affection.

GOLD

...yet shall ye be as the wings of a dove covered with silver, and her feathers with yellow gold.
PSALM 68:13b

Learning to Love

*L*et your mate know he can
trust in your loyalty and fidelity. Trust is one
key to a happy bonding of your love.
Cultivate trust and you cultivate a fulfilling
and refreshing love life.

TRUST

*The heart of her husband doth safely trust in
her, so that he shall have no need of spoil.*
PROVERBS 31:11

Learning to Love

*P*aying homage will bring the shine of love to your mate's eyes. Don't be hesitant to tell of the beauty that is brought to your life by your beloved. Take every opportunity to compliment your loved one.

HOMAGE

Behold, thou art fair, my love; behold, thou art fair; thou hast doves' eyes.
SONG OF SOLOMON 1:15

Learning to Love

*D*on't withhold the sweetness of love from you and your spouse. Accept the delights of love with an open hand. Enjoy and rejoice in the pleasures God has ordained in marriage.

HONEYCOMB

My son, eat thou honey, because it is good; and the honeycomb, which is sweet to thy taste.
PROVERBS 24:13

Learning to Love

*V*irtue is the foundation of a solid marriage. Let your mate know he can safely trust his affection and love to you. Don't give in to the temptation to squander your love in adultery.

VIRTUE

Who can find a virtuous woman? for her price is far above rubies.
PROVERBS 31:10

Learning to Love

*A*n affair begins with the eyes. Be careful not to let your eyes deceive you. The one you desire might look very attractive, but adultery ends in ugly arguments and hidden guilt. What looks pleasant in most cases turns sour and destroys.

WANDERINGS

Better is the sight of the eyes than the wandering of the desire: this is also vanity and vexation of spirit.
ECCLESIASTES 6:9

Learning to Love

*L*ove is like a garden. The seed of love is planted, but unless someone tends the garden a strong plant will never grow. Love requires long, hard work. Today is a good day to start paying attention to your beloved.

GARDEN

...Let my beloved come into his garden and eat his pleasant fruits.
SONG OF SOLOMON 4:16b

Learning to Love

*W*ords can build a relationship or destroy it. Let your words be those that build honesty and love between you and your beloved. Speak from your heart and your love will be healthier for it.

WORDS

Pleasant words are as an honeycomb, sweet to the soul, and health to the bones.
PROVERBS 16:24

Learning to Love

*M*ay your nights be filled with the comfort of a binding love. Don't let the troubles of your day intrude upon the coziness of a night spent in the arms of your beloved.

NIGHTTIME

Come, let us take our fill of love until the morning: let us solace ourselves with loves.
PROVERBS 7:18

15

Learning to Love

*L*ove needs a seal set upon it. A seal says this love of yours is important to you. It says you will be true and faithful to your beloved. Love your mate with confidence.

SEAL

Set me as a seal upon thine heart, as a seal upon thine arm; for love is strong as death...
SONG OF SOLOMON 8:6a

Learning to Love

*K*indness builds love. Act toward your beloved in a kindly manner that seeks the good of the one you love. Show your love by thinking of your mate first — before yourself. You will find a reward beyond your wildest imagination if your love follows this noble path.

KINDLY

And his soul clave unto Dinah the daughter of Jacob, and he loved the damsel, and spake kindly unto the damsel.
GENESIS 34:3

Learning to Love

*T*rue love weathers every storm and outlasts every trouble. Make your love the kind of love that shelters you forever. Build a relationship with your beloved that will comfort you in your old age.

FOREVER

Let her be as the loving hind and pleasant roe; let her breasts satisfy thee at all times; and be thou ravished always with her love.

PROVERBS 5:19

Learning to Love

*A*rguments about money can dim
the pleasure you deserve to have with your
beloved. Discuss with your mate how you
both think your money should be spent. If
you can both agree on a budget, your life
together will be more mutually satisfying.

FINANCES

House and riches are the inheritance of fathers;
and a prudent wife is from the Lord.
PROVERBS 19:14

Learning to Love

*L*oving sex binds a marriage together. Love your spouse unconditionally. Without reserve. Don't use sex as a reward for good behavior or as a threat to get what you want. Love each other abundantly and well.

SEX

The wife hath not power of her own body, but the husband: and likewise also the husband hath not power of his own body, but the wife.

1 CORINTHIANS 7:4

Learning to Love

*S*eek harmony in your relationship with your loved one. Don't take detours to total agreement. Talk about your differences until there is full understanding. Do not be afraid of a healthy compromise. Live with your beloved in peace.

ONE MIND

...Be perfect, be of good comfort, be of one mind, live in peace; and the God of love and peace shall be with you.
II CORINTHIANS 13:11b

Learning to Love

$\mathcal{G}$ood judgment helps pave the way to a lasting and whole relationship with the one you love. Seek wisdom as you live your lives together. If you lack wisdom, ask of God and He will supply your need.

JUDGMENT

And this I pray, that your love may abound yet more and more in knowledge and in all judgment.
PHILIPPIANS 1:9

Learning to Love

*L*ove has a sweet savour. Enjoy the essence of the love you share. Be extravagant often and give yourselves perfumes and ointments that delight the senses. Rejoice in the love of your hearts.

SAVOUR

Ointment and perfume rejoice the heart...
PROVERBS 27:9a

Learning to Love

*M*ake love to your spouse with abandon. God has given you marriage for pleasure as well as for family ties. Enjoy your nights together as much as you cherish your days.

LOVEMAKING

*Marriage is honourable in all, and
the bed undefiled...*
HEBREWS 13:4a

Learning to Love

*D*o not yield to the temptation to take another into your arms. Adultery may seem a pleasant diversion, but the end result can be the death of a marriage. Be true to the one you love and relish in your mate's uniqueness and beauty.

LUST

But every man is tempted, when he is drawn away of his own lust, and enticed. Then when lust hath conceived, it bringeth forth sin: and sin, when it is finished, bringeth forth death.

JAMES 1.14,15

Learning to Love

*P*ut actions behind your sweet
words of love. Don't just say "I love you,"
show your beloved how much you care.
Look for things you can do to please your
mate—*every day.*

ACTIONS

*My little children, let us not love in word,
neither in tongue; but in deed and in truth.*
I JOHN 3:18

Learning to Love

*G*od is the One who joined you together with your beloved. He is the one who ordained marriage between a man and a woman. If you need guidance in your marriage — and you will — ask it from the One who abundantly and freely gives.

BONDED

...For this cause shall a man leave father and mother, and shall cleave to his wife... What therefore God hath joined together, let not man put asunder.

MATTHEW 19.5,6

Learning to Love

*B*e patient in your love. Don't insist on returning a harsh word that has been spoken. Don't always try to make the last parting shot in an argument. Love your spouse even when your mate is not acting in love.

AFFECTION

For if ye love them which love you, what reward have ye? do not even the publicans the same? Be ye therefore perfect, even as your Father which is in heaven is perfect.
MATTHEW 5:46,48

Learning to Love

*I*f you feel you need strength to continue to love your mate, don't despair. God has promised to give His all encompassing strength to those who ask it of Him. So be patient and prayerfully wait.

UP LIFT

Wait on the Lord: be of good courage, and he shall strengthen thine heart: wait, I say, on the Lord.

PSALM 27:14

29

Learning to Love

*G*uard your heart against the possibility of an adulterous affair. Don't even fantasize about having an affair. The fantasy is the first step toward a reality that could destroy your marriage.

FANTASY

Ye have heard that it was said by them of old time: Thou shalt not commit adultery: But I say unto you, That whosoever looketh on a woman to lust after her hath committed adultery with her already in his heart.
MATTHEW 5:27,28

Learning to Love

*D*evelop God-like patterns in your
life with your beloved. Ask yourself how
God would like you to treat your mate.
Never settle for less. Be kind, be patient, be
filled with a loving mercy.

PATTERNS

*Be ye therefore merciful, as your
Father also is merciful.*
LUKE 6:36

Learning to Love

A spouse's conversation can be like the sound of constant dripping water—nagging and irritating. Or it can gladden the heart like a bubbling stream. Let your words be ever pleasant.

CONVERSATION

Likewise ye wives, be in subjection to your own husbands; that, if any obey not the word, they also may without the word be won by the conversation of the wives.
I PETER 3:1

Growing Together

*G*od crowns each year of our life with His goodness. His mercy and love cushion us from life's hard blows. His care goes before us and He prepares a way for us through all our days.

GOODNESS

Thou crownest the year with thy goodness, and thy paths drop fatness.
PSALM 65:11

Growing Together

*A*s a new day begins, remember
God has brought you and your loved one
together for a life of joy and fruitfulness.
Don't settle for less.

FRUITFULNESS

*They shall still bring forth fruit in old age; they
shall be fat and flourishing.*
PSALM 92:14

Growing Together

Thank God for your friends and family. The bonds of love that draw you to each other are blessed by God. He wants you to rejoice in the ties of love He has given you.

FAMILIES

God setteth the solitary in families: he bringeth out those which are bound with chains: but the rebellious dwell in a dry land.

PSALM 68:6

Growing Together

*P*rayer cements your heart to the heart of your beloved. Take time to pray with the special one you love. In praying, you draw near to the soul of the one who means so much to you.

PRAYER

For where two or three are gathered together in my name, there am I in the midst of them.
MATTHEW 18:20

Growing Together

*L*ove has its price. When you stand with your beloved, you can not always stand with the rest of the world. But it is the willingness to make this choice that is a sign of true love.

CHOICES

Therefore shall a man leave his father and his mother and shall cleave unto his wife: and they shall be one flesh.
GENESIS 2:24

Growing Together

*E*mbrace your beloved with a joyful heart. Be happy and delight in the smile, the kiss, and the love of the one who rules your heart. Let your joy shine in your eyes and be evident in the words of your mouth.

JOYFUL

Let the field be joyful, and all that is therein:
then shall all the trees of the wood rejoice.
PSALM 96:12

Growing Together

*Y*our love grows from a seed that God planted in your heart. No one succeeds in truly loving another unless God gives him or her the ability. It's God who makes your love flourish. Remember Him in worship and prayer.

SEED

Those that be planted in the house of the Lord shall flourish in the courts of our God.
PSALM 92:13

Growing Together

*L*ying in bed with your loved one keeps you warm through all of life's seasons. When you are together in your intimacy, you can forget the storms that rage outside. So draw near to each other and be warm.

WARMTH

Again, if two lie together, then they have heat: but how can one be warm alone?
ECCLESIASTES 4:11

Growing Together

*Y*ou and your beloved both grow as you seek to know God better. Don't be content with a glimpse of Him. Search the Scriptures and yearn to see His face clearly. He'll show Himself to those that seek Him.

SEEK

Seek the Lord, and his strength: seek his face evermore.
PSALM 105:4

Growing Together

*G*od promises you peace as you draw near to Him. When you are bitter or angry, don't keep your feelings to yourself. Talk about them with a friend. Then bring your concerns to a God who loves you. He will give you peace.

PEACE

Great peace have they which love thy law: and nothing shall offend them.
PSALM 119:165

Growing Together

*S*hare your troubles with your beloved. Together you can work to turn your troubles into triumphs. No one is able to do alone what two can do together, especially when it comes to prayer.

SHARING

And Isaac intreated with the Lord for his wife, because she was barren: and the Lord was intreated of him, and Rebekah his wife conceived.

GENESIS 25:21

Growing Together

*D*on't neglect the reading of God's word with your beloved. Spending time together getting to know God better is one of the richest joys you will know as a couple. His word will delight and strengthen you.

SCRIPTURE

Thy word is very pure: therefore thy servant loveth it.
PSALM 119:140

Growing Together

*G*od blesses the pleasure you share
with the one you have married. Savour the
sweetness of sleeping in your beloved's
arms. Carry the sweetness into the day, let
it be a comfort to you.

PLEASURE

*A bundle of myrrh is my well-beloved unto me,
he shall lie all night betwixt my breasts.*
SONG OF SOLOMON 1:13

Growing Together

*G*od made you to love and be loved
by those of the opposite sex, from your
parent to teenage friends to the one who
has become your mate. Rejoice in the
maleness of men and the
femaleness of women.

CREATED

*...from the beginning of the creation God made
them male and female.*
MARK 10:6

Growing Together

*O*ne of the joys and mysteries of
life is the way in which a man and a
woman can become one. The two come
together physically, emotionally, and
spiritually. They are no longer two:
they are one.

ONE

*And they twain shall be one flesh: so then they
are no more twain, but one flesh.*
MARK 10·8

Growing Together

 ncontrollable anger can destroy love. Learn to make your anger a tool to resolve problems rather than let it become a problem in and of itself. Don't let anger build inside until you explode. Handle each day's disagreements within the day itself.

DISAGREEMENTS

He that is slow to anger is better than the mighty; and he that ruleth his spirit than he that taketh a city.
PROVERBS 16:32

Growing Together

*P*ower and love — how do they mix? Each couple needs to pray and consider how they are to relate to one another. Without love, power is harsh. When there is love, there is no need for power.

POWER

But I would have you know, that the head of every man is Christ; and the head of the woman is the man; and the head of Christ is God.

1 CORINTHIANS 11:3

Growing Together

*L*ove doesn't stay the same. It shrinks
and it expands. Encourage love to grow so
that the love you share with your mate
tomorrow, next month or next year, is
larger and greater than the love
you share today.

MULTIPLY

*Mercy unto you, and peace, and love,
be multiplied.*
JUDE 2

Growing Together

$\mathcal{G}$od made wedding vows as strong as steel and as fragile as cut glass. Protect and honor the promises you've made to your beloved. Don't let anyone come between you and your spouse.

JOINED

*What therefore God hath joined together,
let not man put asunder.*
MARK 10:9

Growing Together

*L*earn to hold your loved one tightly. Don't take the one you love for granted. Tell your beloved of your feelings. Love is a precious gift and needs to be cherished. Say "I love you" today.

CLEAVE

For this cause shall a man leave his father and mother, and cleave to his wife.

MARK 10:7

Growing Together

*W*hen others criticize your beloved, don't join in. Be supportive of your mate. Temper any of your own criticisms with the solid assurance that you are on your lover's side.

CRITICS

And if one prevail against him, two shall withstand him...
ECCLESIASTES 4:12a

Growing Together

*L*ove your mate abundantly. Be generous and tell your beloved often of your love. Tell others that you love this very special person. Let your love shine in your eyes and be demonstrated in your words.

BANNER

He brought me to the banqueting house, and his banner over me was love.
SONG OF SOLOMON 2:4

Growing Together

*A*s you grow to know your beloved, grow also to know the Lord who watches over both of you. Spend time meditating on the Word of God. Do not be content with only a surface knowledge of the Savior. Dig deeply into the riches of His presence.

SATISFIED

As for me, I will behold thy face in righteousness; I shall be satisfied when I awake, with thy likeness.
PSALM 17:15

Growing Together

*I*f you have made a major mistake in your relationship with your beloved, don't despair. Be thankful, it's always possible to begin anew. Ask your mate for forgiveness and a clean slate. With God's help, you can and will enjoy an even more fruitful and satisfying life together.

RENEWAL

Create in me a clean heart, O God, and renew a right spirit within me.
PSALM 51:10

Growing Together

*S*peak honestly to your mate. Don't be politely silent when hurt and anger pulse through your veins. Honest words spoken in love make your relationship grow and flourish.

HONESTY

The words of his mouth were smoother than butter, but war was in his heart; his words were softer than oil, yet were they drawn swords.

Growing Together

*T*ake time to enjoy your beloved.
Refresh your spirit and your love with time
together in a quiet, special place. Forget
your troubles for a moment and speak only
of the love you share.

EACH OTHER

*As the apple tree among the trees of the wood,
so is my beloved among the sons. I sat down
under his shadow with great delight, and his
fruit was sweet to my taste.*
SONG OF SOLOMON 2:3

Growing Together

*D*on't try to hold your marriage together by yourself. Ask God for His grace and mercy on your union. God specializes in healing broken hearts. He brings His oil of love and kindness to households where peace is in short supply.

MERCY

But I am like a green olive tree in the house of God: I trust in the mercy of God for ever and ever.

PSALM 52:8

Growing Together

*L*ove draws you close to your beloved until the lines that separate you grow indistinct. God's Word says that marriage vows bring people together until they are flesh of the same flesh and bone of the same bone.

FLESH

And Adam said, 'This is now bone of my bones, and flesh of my flesh: she shall be called Woman, because she was taken out of Man.'
GENESIS 2:23

Growing Together

*R*iches do not bring happiness.
Finding peace with your beloved will.
Expensive presents will never make up for
unloving actions. Learn to love with your
actions and not with your wallet
or purse alone.

HANDS FILLED

Better is an handful with quietness, than both
the hands full with travail and
vexation of spirit.
ECCLESIASTES 4:6

Growing Together

*L*ove's first breath can be sweet. But true love grows with the years until the first part of love is only a shadow of the real tie that binds a couple together after a lifetime of love.

ENDINGS

Better is the end of a thing than the beginning thereof: and the patient in spirit is better than the proud in spirit.

ECCLESIASTES 7:8

Comforting Each Other

*Y*ou don't need to bear your troubles all alone. Speak openly to your beloved about the deepest concerns of your heart. Then together go to God in prayer, asking Him to lift your burden and ease your anxiety. Let a gracious and loving Savior help you with your every challenge.

TOGETHER

Cast thy burden upon the Lord, And He shall sustain thee...
PSALM 55:22a

Comforting Each Other

*H*old your mate tightly when trouble enters your relationship and begins to shake your lives. Don't be afraid to cry and to feel your feelings to their very edges. God made you *and* your emotions and put them into one body called YOU! Tears cleanse. Frustration when dealt with in love can bring about healing. God also wants you to tell Him how you feel so He can provide for you the comfort He promises.

MOURN

Blessed are they that mourn: for they shall be comforted.
MATTHEW 5:4

Comforting Each Other

*D*on't comfort your beloved from a standpoint of weakness. Be strong. Have courage. Speak the truth in love. Comfort your spouse in a way that brings encouragement. Help build on strengths that already exist Remember life has many seasons and troubles come and go. You always have reason to hope.

ENCOURAGEMENT

Wherefore comfort yourselves together, and edify one another, even as also ye do.
I THESSALONIANS 5:11

Comforting Each Other

*G*od doesn't ask you to have blind trust in Him. He knows your troubles and that their pain often overwhelms you. That's why He offers you and your beloved a refuge, an everpresent haven during the stormy times. Come to Him together in prayer and let Him give you the delight of His own heart.

REFUGE

Trust in Him at all times, ye people, pour out your heart before Him; God is a refuge for us. Selah.
PSALM 62:8

Comforting Each Other

*D*on't give up hope when the dreams you have for you and your beloved seem to appear impossible. God specializes in making the impossible possible. He enjoys helping you make your dreams come true. Talk to Him about what is on your heart. Do it now.

IMPOSSIBLE

And Jesus looking upon them saith, With men it is impossible, but not with God: for with God all things are possible.
MARK 10:27

Comforting Each Other

*W*hen you find it difficult to be patient because of conflicts you're experiencing with your mate, remember God has asked you to maintain your love relationship in spite of these challenges. Be patient and help ease the troubles of the one you love. Read I Corinthians 13 to help you put your relationship back on course.

SUBMISSION

Wives, submit yourselves unto your own husbands, as unto the Lord...Husbands, love your wives, even as Christ also loved the church, and gave Himself for it.
EPHESIANS 5:22,25

Comforting Each Other

*C*omfort your beloved with words of
understanding and cheer. Don't be one to
focus your conversation on your troubles.
God loves a cheerful heart...and so will the
one with whom you live.

CHEER

Heaviness in the heart of man maketh it stoop:
but a good word maketh it glad.
PROVERBS 12:25

Comforting Each Other

*W*hen you are feeling sad, take a few moments to remember how God has worked in the life of you and your beloved in the past. Take comfort from the past successes you have enjoyed together.

THE PAST

I remembered thy judgments of old, O Lord; and have comforted myself.
PSALM 119:52

Comforting Each Other

*Y*ou never need to fix the pieces of a broken heart alone. Take your sadness to friends and especially to that friend who sticks closer than a brother, Jesus Christ. He promises to heal the wounds of those who call Him Lord.

HEALING

The Lord is nigh unto them that are of a broken heart...
PSALM 34:18a

Comforting Each Other

*W*hen you feel inadequate because you feel you cannot ease the pain of your beloved, remember God is the One who brings about the healing of body and spirit. Bring your beloved to Him in earnest prayer. God is faithful and promises to listen to your most desperate plea.

INADEQUATE

For a certain woman, whose young daughter had an unclean spirit, heard of him, and came and fell at his feet...And when she was come to her house, she found the devil gone out, and her daughter laid upon the bed.

MARK 7:25,30

Comforting Each Other

*E*very marriage has its own special ups and downs. No man or woman has ever been perfect in his or her love. As you recognize your own humanity, ask God to take the hurts in your relationship and show you and your beloved how to turn your greatest challenges into triumphs.

GLADNESS

Thou hast turned for me my mourning into dancing: Thou hast put off my sackcloth, and girded me with gladness.

PSALM 30:11

Comforting Each Other

*H*old your spouse closely when you face grief together. Weep together over your losses. But remember that God is able to turn your night of darkness into a wonderful, fulfilling morning of light and joy.

MORNING

...Weeping may endure for a night, but joy cometh in the morning.
PSALM 30:5b

Comforting Each Other

*T*he death of a loving parent can shake you and your beloved to your core. It may be extremely difficult to accept this great loss. However, as you and your spouse grieve together, be thankful to a merciful God that He has given you someone to share your deepest pain.

DEATH

Then Isaac brought her into his mother Sarah's tent, and took Rebekah, and she became his wife; and he loved her: and Isaac was comforted after his mother's death.
GENESIS 24:67

Comforting Each Other

*S*ometimes the heartaches in your life will seem like they are simply too much to bear. But never forget that you and your mate have a special hiding place. The Word of God promises you that your heavenly Father comforts and hides His children under His wings.

HIDING

Keep me as the apple of the eye; hide me under the shadow of Thy wings.
PSALM 17:8

Comforting Each Other

*G*od never suggested He would take away all your burdens in life. You and your beloved will both struggle until the day you die. That is simply the formula known as life! But God has promised to make your burdens lighter, never to give you more than you can bear, and to give you His divine rest as you carry them.

REST

Come unto me, all ye that labour and are heavy laden, and I will give you rest.
MATTHEW 11:28

Comforting Each Other

*S*ometimes you will have to do things
that may frighten you. Perhaps you'll need
to change jobs, move to a new city, or
move out of your "comfort zone" to take
on a brand new challenge. Be brave and
live today and always in the awareness that
you can be confident God goes before you
and will give you the strength you need.

BRAVERY

*Be of good courage, and he shall strengthen
your heart, all ye that hope in the Lord.*
PSALM 31:24

Comforting Each Other

*A*s you and your beloved grow to maturity, you will see that it was during the really *tough times* that you developed your stability, resolve and inner strength. Be comforted in your troubles because that is one way in which an all-knowing God shapes and perfects you.

MATURITY

Now no chastening for the present seemeth to be joyous, but grievous: nevertheless afterward it yieldeth the peaceable fruit of righteousness unto them which are exercised thereby.

HEBREWS 12:11

Comforting Each Other

*D*on't just count on seeing God's fair treatment in heaven. The Psalmist says God works justice in our earthly lives as well. In the *here and now*! Ask a just and loving God to work in your life and to keep you faithful to Him at all times.
Whatever the cost.

FAIR TREATMENT

I had fainted, unless I had believed to see the goodness of the Lord in the land of the living.
PSALM 27:13

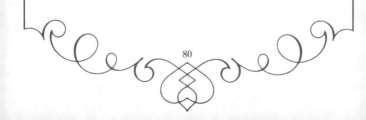

Comforting Each Other

*I*n the stress and challenges of life, sometimes you may forget that your physical presence is a comfort to your mate. Make it a point to be with your beloved in person when you know your loved one is going through difficult times.

HOME

When a man hath taken a new wife, he shall not go out to war, neither shall he be charged with any business; but he shall be free at home one year, and shall cheer up his wife which he hath taken.

DEUTERONOMY 24:5

Comforting Each Other

*I*t's a physical law—your life is going to be filled with alterations both good and bad. God is able to work in every circumstance of your life. Sadness may be for a night but joy, fulfillment and comfort will visit you in the morning.

ALTERATION

To every thing there is a season, and a time to every purpose under the heaven...a time to embrace, and a time to refrain from embracing, A time to get, and a time to lose...
ECCLESIASTES 3:1,5b,6a

Comforting Each Other

*A*t times you may wonder if God is either sleeping or dead. Well, don't despair. The Psalmist reminds us that God never sleeps nor slumbers. He is always awake, attentive and aware of the trials that face you. Start trusting Him in a new way. Start this new adventure today!

WATCHFUL

He will not suffer thy foot to be moved: He that keepeth thee will not slumber.
PSALM 121:3

Comforting Each Other

*D*on't engage in excessive worry about your daily needs. God watches over all His creation and He sees and knows what is vital for your sustenance. Come to Him with your beloved and tell Him of the things you need each day. Come to Him in faith — believing He will do what He promises.

NEEDS

Wherefore, if God so clothe the grass of the field, which today is, and tomorrow is cast into the oven, shall He not much more clothe you, O ye of little faith?
MATTHEW 6:30

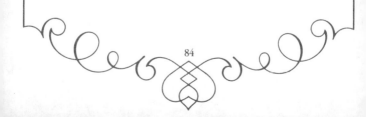

Comforting Each Other

*S*ometimes it may feel like God is very far away from you and the ones you hold dear. But in reality, God is near at hand no matter where you are — from the top of the highest mountain to the bottom of the deepest ocean. Remember His promise...*I will never leave you nor forsake you.* Live in that awareness of His closeness to you.

CLOSER

If I take the wings of the morning, and dwell in the uttermost parts of the sea; Even there shall thy hand lead me, and thy right hand shall hold me.
PSALM 139:9,10

Comforting Each Other

*W*hen you are unhappy, imagine
yourself being held tightly in the arms of
God your Father. Sometimes you must travel
deep into the valley of tears before you can
begin to scale the great mountain of joy.
Remember, unhappiness does not
last forever.

TEARS

They that sow in tears shall reap in joy.
PSALM 126:5

Comforting Each Other

*N*ew life arises out of sorrow. As you comfort yourself and your beloved, think about how you can redeem your hard times. Learn to bring good out of what for the moment seems bad. Adapt your thinking to that of the Apostle Paul...and be content in whatever circumstances you and your spouse find yourselves.

REDEEM

And David comforted Bathsheba his wife, and went in unto her, and lay with her: and she bare a son, and he called his name Solomon: and the Lord loved him.
II SAMUEL 12:24

Comforting Each Other

*T*hroughout history people have asked God, "Why, Lord, why?". You are not alone if you feel yourself asking this question day after day. Be bold and free enough to ask God to give you understanding of His deepest mysteries.

WHY?

That their hearts might be comforted, being knit together in love, and unto all riches of the full assurance of understanding, to the acknowledgement of the mystery of God, and of the Father, and of Christ.

COLOSSIANS 2:2

Comforting Each Other

*L*oneliness can weigh heavily on you when you face a difficult decision. If you and your mate cannot agree on the path you are about to take, agree to disagree without pulling away from each other.

AGREEMENT

Reproach hath broken my heart; and I am full of heaviness: and I looked for some to take pity, but there was none; and for comforters, but I found none.

PSALM 69:20

Comforting Each Other

$\mathcal{B}$e fierce in your loyalty to your mate. Don't let others belittle the one you love. Show your beloved that you can be counted on no matter what situations arise.

PRESENCE

So Jonathan arose from the table in fierce anger, and did eat no meat the second day of the month: for he was grieved for David, because his father had done him shame.

I SAMUEL 20:34

Comforting Each Other

*G*od promises you and your beloved a safe dwelling place in Him. Bring your hurts and disappointments to your Loving Father who wants only His best for you. Don't try to face life all on your own. Live your life by living and loving *together.*

SAFETY

But whoso hearkeneth unto me shall dwell safely, and shall be quiet from fear of evil.
PROVERBS 1:33

Comforting Each Other

$\mathcal{G}$rief and loss come to all of us. You and your spouse are no exception. When you sense your life is empty and you are discouraged, talk with God — and with your mate — about how you feel and discuss ways in which you can rise above the circumstances and meet life head-on with joy and enthusiasm.

DISCOURAGEMENT

I am weary of my crying: my throat is dried: mine eyes fail while I wait for my God.
PSALM 69:3

Comforting Each Other

*S*ay "I love you" often to your spouse. Many hearts have grown dry waiting to hear those three precious words. Say them often with deep feeling and they will make your relationship a refreshing oasis in the desert.

REFRESHMENT

Repent ye therefore, and be converted, that your sins may be blotted out, when the times of refreshing shall come from the presence of the Lord.

ACTS 3:19

Accepting One Another

*L*ove captivates the beloved and holds it with soft bonds of affection. Thoughts of personal desires and freedom pale beside the promise of plunging to the depths of another's heart and spirit. This is what true, self-giving love is all about.

CAPTIVATES

I am my beloved's, and my beloved is mine...
SONG OF SOLOMON 6:3a

Accepting One Another

*R*esentment and unresolved anger slices through love. It afflicts wounds that may take a lifetime of recovery. Give up those grudges that may one day turn to cold anger. Tell your beloved how you feel and seek to live together in peace.

PEACE

...The LORD will bless His people with peace.
PSALM 29:11b

Accepting One Another

*T*rust is built when two people keep and cherish each other's secrets. Protect your beloved's privacy with the same care you use to guard your own. Show your faithfulness to your mate in this manner.

PRIVACY

A talebearer revealeth secrets: but he that is of a faithful spirit concealeth the matter.
PROVERBS 11:13

Accepting One Another

*T*rue love doesn't keep score of the wrongs of another. If you continue to tally the wrongs of your beloved and refuse to let go of the past, you simply cannot grow into a relationship filled with grace and forgiveness. Forgive and forget. You will both be the winners in the long run.

WRONGS

If thou, LORD, shouldest mark iniquities, O Lord, who shall stand? But there is forgiveness with thee,...
PSALM 130:3,4a

Accepting One Another

*T*rue love must stretch like rubber
when personal growth begins to take place.
Give your beloved room to be God's whole,
complete person. Be an encouragement
and not a discouragement. Recognize that
change is an important
part of development.

CHANGE

*Charity suffereth long, and is kind; charity
envieth not; charity vaunteth not itself, is
not puffed up.*
1 CORINTHIANS 13:4

Accepting One Another

*G*od is the judge of your actions. He will either reward or discipline you for your deeds. Don't waste time acting as judge, jury and executioner of your beloved's actions. God will deliver His own appropriate justice to all people. Your task is to love, listen and care for the one you love.

JUSTICE

But God is the judge: he putteth down one, and setteth up another.
PSALM 75:7

Accepting One Another

*L*ove is the balm that helps ease the friction of life between two people who have made a lifelong commitment to each other's growth and development. You and your spouse are not the same. That's what drew you together in the first place. Don't let irritation spoil the months of pleasure you have with your beloved. Apply the healing balm of love often. Start right now.

IRRITATION

...the contentions of a wife are a continual dropping.
PROVERBS 19:13b

Accepting One Another

*T*ruth is a precious gift given freely to you and your beloved. It's simply yours for the taking. Telling the truth is the key to being known by each other and feeling the wondrous release of being wholly approved of by your beloved. With true approval lies great peace.

APPROVAL

Charity...Rejoiceth not in iniquity, but rejoiceth in the truth;
1 CORINTHIANS 13:4a,6

Accepting One Another

*Y*our words of love are of more value than the costliest pearls. Give your love words freely to your beloved. Don't let a lack of self confidence or doubt rob you and your beloved of the joy of sharing expressions that speak of romance and affection.

VALUE

Even a fool, when he holdeth his peace, is counted wise: and he that shutteth his lips is esteemed a man of understanding.
PROVERBS 17:28

Accepting One Another

*K*indness must be weaved through
the fabric of the love you hold for your
beloved. This thread must be strong
enough to hold the more fragile emotions
together. Seek to be kind to your mate.
Look for special ways to be gentle and
sensitive. Together you can weather
any storm.

KINDNESS

*And be ye kind one to another, tenderhearted,
forgiving one another, even as God for Christ's
sake hath forgiven you.*
EPHESIANS 4:32

Accepting One Another

*U*nresolved anger opens wounds and causes pain to spread throughout the relationship with your spouse. Cleanse your wounds before anger can take over. Be honest with your feelings. Anger is based on hurt, fear or frustration. Deal with the real issues — in truth and love.

ANGER

It is better to dwell in the wilderness, than with a contentious and an angry woman.
PROVERBS 21:19

Accepting One Another

*F*ill your mind with wondrous thoughts of the good things God has given you and your beloved — the life you share, the love that draws you to each other — the faith that helps you grow.

THOUGHTS

Finally, brethren, whatsoever things are true, whatsoever things are honest, whatsoever things are just, whatsoever things are pure, whatsoever things are lovely, whatsoever things are of good report; if there be any virtue, and if there be any praise, think on these things.

PHILIPPIANS 4:8

Accepting One Another

*L*ove can easily be clouded over with discouragement and despair. Sometimes you will find yourself confused, not knowing which direction to turn for help in your relationship. The good news is that God promises to give you His understanding in all matters. Lean on Him for His mercy and guidance.

UNDERSTANDING

If any of you lack wisdom, let him ask of God, that giveth to all men liberally, and upbraideth not; and it shall be given him.

JAMES 1:5

Accepting One Another

*L*ove is a dance of poetry. Each lover bows to the other and says "No, please, you go first." Bring the poetry of *"you first"* back into your relationship with your beloved. Out-do each other showing love one for the other. It will sweeten your love and make it stronger.

ESTEEM

Let nothing be done through strife or vainglory; but in lowliness of mind let each esteem other better than themselves.
PHILIPPIANS 2:3

Accepting One Another

*Y*ou and your beloved stand naked before your Father in Heaven, stripped of your defenses, apologies and excuses. He sees — and miraculously loves — the real untarnished YOU! Give thanks for His acceptance.

DEFENSELESS

And above all things have fervent charity among yourselves: for charity shall cover the multitude of sins.
I PETER 4:8

Accepting One Another

*G*od has a cozy place for you and
your spouse in His Fatherly heart. When
you are sad, He invites you to come to Him
and share your every burden. He will share
His heart with you and give you peace.
Come into His heart today and
feel His love.

HEART

...God is love; and he that dwelleth in love
dwelleth in God, and God in him.
I JOHN 4:16b

Accepting One Another

*R*emember the first recognition of mutual love you shared with your beloved — the excitement, the rush of ecstasy, the tingle of fear. Rekindle the passion of those first moments of love. Treat your spouse as kindly today as you did on your first date. You just may be amazed at the response.

REKINDLE

Nevertheless I have somewhat against thee, because thou hast left thy first love.
REVELATION 2:4

Accepting One Another

*L*ove is wonderfully contagious. God's loving kindness to you can prompt you to acts of loving kindness to your spouse. Let your whole household be infected with the joy of loving. Spread that joy today— wherever you are and in whatever you do.

CONTAGIOUS

Beloved, if God so loved us, we ought also to love one another.
1 JOHN 4:11

Accepting One Another

*T*he path of love often leads through webs of pain and hope often unobserved by others. Your private fears and dreams are yours alone until you share them with that special one you love. Explore unseen places gently.

UNSEEN

There is a path which no fowl knoweth, and which the vulture's eye hath not seen.
JOB 28:7

Accepting One Another

*T*rue love has weak eyesight. Faults
are not seen and imperfections not noted.
So open your life wide to the forgiving eyes
of your beloved. Only in openness is
knowing one another possible.

FORGIVING

For every tree is known by his own fruit...
LUKE 6:44a

Accepting One Another

*A*sk God to spread His light of love around the hearts of you and your beloved. His light will be the laser beam of Truth that helps you know each other in your innermost being. Delve deeply to the core of your togetherness. Such knowing is the foundation of love.

INNERMOST

When his candle shined upon my head, and when by his light I walked through darkness.
JOB 29:3

Accepting One Another

*W*oo your beloved with affectionate words and pleasing ways. Drink your mate's refreshing nectar. Seek to know your spouse more deeply every day you share together. Recognize the value of your every moment together. A relationship filled with love makes you a wealthy couple indeed.

BENEFITS

Blessed be the Lord, who daily loadeth us with benefits, even the God of our Salvation. Selah.
PSALM 68:19

Accepting One Another

 *G*od has provided marriage as one way for His children to grow to perfection. When someone knows you as well as your spouse, you can always run...*but you can never hide!* Use your learning about one another to encourage growth.

PERFECTION

Wherefore, beloved, seeing that ye look for such things, be diligent that ye may be found of Him in peace, without spot, and blameless.
II PETER 3:14

Accepting One Another

*T*roubles can steal the seeds of your marital happiness before you can plant them. Fight the troubles. Store the seeds well. Together with your mate, ask God to help you overcome all your difficulties. He is faithful to grant you His counsel and wisdom. Take advantage of it.

FIGHT

The Lord your God which goeth before you, He shall fight for you,...
DEUTERONOMY 1:30a

Accepting One Another

*L*ove is a powerful persuader and seducer. Use your love to draw your mate closer to the heart of the One True God. Guard your own faith so your mate does not entice you away from Him.

ENTICEMENT

If thy brother,...or the wife of thy bosom, or thy friend, which is as thine own soul, entice thee secretly, saying Let us go and serve other gods, which thou hast not known, thou, nor thy fathers; ...Thou shalt not consent unto him...

DEUTERONOMY 13:6a,8a

Accepting One Another

*B*uild your marriage upon the sure foundation of a shared faith and hope in the Lord Jesus Christ. If you and your beloved are aiming at the same targets, and moving toward the same goals, your opportunities for growth and fulfillment are magnified many times over.

FOUNDATION

Therefore whosoever heareth these sayings of mine, and doeth them, I will liken him unto a wise man, which built his house upon a rock:

MATTHEW 7:24

Accepting One Another

*W*hen you lie in your bed at night, loneliness may sometimes flood your soul even though your mate is lying by your side. See this as your inner yearning for the God who promises to fill your innermost being with joy.

LONGINGS

My soul breaketh for the longing that it hath unto thy judgments at all times.

PSALM 119:20

Accepting One Another

*S*ow seeds of righteousness and joy in your relationship with your beloved mate. Cultivate happiness together. God will cause the seeds to grow to full bloom when you make Him first in your lives.

PLANTING

For as the earth bringeth forth her bud, and as the garden causeth the things that are sown in it to spring forth; so the Lord God will cause righteousness and praise to spring forth before all the nations.

ISAIAH 61:11

Accepting One Another

*E*njoy all of the pleasures of the senses with your beloved. Walk together on a balmy afternoon. Enjoy a stroll in the gentle rain. Put the cares of business aside and make a date with your spouse today. After all, your beloved *is* the most important person in your life.

NATURE

The flowers appear on the earth; the time of the singing of birds is come, and the voice of the turtle is heard in our land.
SONG OF SOLOMON 2:12

Accepting One Another

*S*trive to look at yourself clearly. God has given you a multitude of gifts and talents. He has given perhaps similar — and perhaps much different — talents to your mate. Encourage yourself and your spouse to develop all the talents God has given you both. Do the very best with the equipment you have. It's all you'll ever need.

TALENT

And unto one he gave five talents, to another two, and to another one: to every man according to his several ability; and straightway took his journey.
MATTHEW 25:15

Being Companions

*L*ove has many dimensions and can make you more scattered or more centered. Concentrate and seek to be of one mind with your mate. Discuss what you both want from your relationship and then pull together to reach that goal.

CONCENTRATE

Finally, be ye all of one mind, having compassion one of another, love as brethren, be pitiful, be courteous.
I PETER 3:8

Being Companions

*Y*our love relationship orbits around God even as the moon moves around the earth. God keeps your relationship moving, fluid and dynamic. Always remember that your heavenly Father is the One behind all the love you give and receive.

MOVEMENT

For thou, O God, hast proved us: thou hast tried us, as silver is tried.

PSALM 66:10

Being Companions

*S*avour the companionship you share with your beloved. Breathe deeply of the beautiful fragrance of your love. Rejoice in the blessings you enjoy as a couple.

REJOICE

Let thy fountain be blessed: and rejoice with the wife of thy youth.
PROVERBS 5:18

Being Companions

*T*he first taste of love can strike you like a thunderbolt. But it's the steady, constant companionship and friendship that makes that first exhaustive moment of passion grow into a love to endure for a lifetime. Grow with your beloved.

INCREASE

And the Lord make you to increase and abound in love one toward another,...
1 THESSALONIANS 3:12a

Being Companions

*Y*ou and your beloved are intertwined. The love you have for each other shines all around you —and the world smiles at your devotion. Keep your love shining. Never betray the love you share with your mate.

BETRAYAL

A virtuous woman is a crown to her husband: but she that maketh ashamed is as rottenness in his bones.

PROVERBS 12:4

Being Companions

*D*eep in the soul of every man and woman is the desire to know God and experience His divine love. Honor that desire in your mate and make God the cornerstone of your marriage.

SALVATION

Let all those that seek thee rejoice and be glad in thee: and let such as love thy salvation say continually, Let God be magnified.

PSALM 70:4

Being Companions

*L*ive in the heart of your beloved. Risk romance with the one you love. Speak the poetry of your love even if the words don't seem like polished gems to you. Your lover will treasure the words.

ROMANCE

Then she said, Let me find favour in thy sight, my lord; for that thou hast comforted me, and for that thou has spoken friendly unto thine handmaid, though I be not like unto one of thine handmaidens.

RUTH 2:13

Being Companions

*G*od sees the hidden heart of everyone. Give your innermost thoughts to God in prayer. Let Him help you and your mate separate the good from the bad that you might be more fruitful for Him.

SEPARATION

The Lord looked down from heaven upon the children of men, to see if there were any that did understand, and seek God.

PSALM 14:2

Being Companions

*C*ry out to God when you feel lonely. Loneliness can engulf you and leave you floating on an endless sea of despair. Ask God to bring you comfort and trust Him to help you.

CRY

Lover and friend hast thou put far from me, and mine acquaintance into darkness.
PSALM 88:18

Being Companions

*L*ove has many faces. Its most beautiful countenance is the face of friendship. Cultivate a deep, lasting friendship with your beloved. Play together with abandon, share your interests, take long walks and learn to be one heart in two bodies.

FRIENDSHIP

A friend loveth at all times,...
PROVERBS 17:17a

Being Companions

*W*hen you love, your soul meets and kisses the good that is inside the soul of your beloved. Nurture that which is righteous, correct and noble in your beloved...and let your beloved encourage those same qualities within you.

RIGHTEOUS

Mercy and truth are met together; righteousness and peace have kissed each other.
PSALM 85:10

Being Companions

*C*ONFIDENTIAL should be stamped across your love relationship in large red letters. The privacy you give your beloved makes it possible to tell of your innermost thoughts, feeling secure in the knowledge that they will be safe with your mate.

CONFIDENTIAL

He that covereth a transgression seeketh love; but he that repeateth a matter separateth very friends.
PROVERBS 17:9

Being Companions

*T*rue love doesn't worry about who's the boss. It doesn't keep score in the "who's turn is it now" game. True love rejoices in doing what is good for your beloved and in serving one another.

SERVANTHOOD

But he that is greatest among you shall be your servant.
MATTHEW 23:11

Being Companions

True love knits two people together until the threads of one life are intertwined with the threads of the other. Celebrate the unity you share with the mate God has given you. Give thanks today — right now — by praising God for what you are sharing together.

UNITY

Behold, how good and how pleasant it is for brethren to dwell together in unity!
PSALM 133:1

Being Companions

*A*ny romantic relationship falters at times...and only a more mature, wiser person can tell you how to rekindle your love. Seek help from others when you do not know how to mend a troubled relationship. Help is near. Be courageous enough to seek it.

COUNSEL

Where no counsel is, the people fall: but in the multitude of counsellors there is safety.
PROVERBS 11:14

Being Companions

$\mathscr{P}$oets have tried for centuries to capture the essence of love. The Bible tells us quite simply that real love is caring more about others than you care for yourself and your own needs. Be a model of selfless love in your relationship. It will be contagious.

LOVE

Nevertheless let every one of you in particular so love his wife even as himself; and the wife see that she reverence her husband.

EPHESIANS 5:33

Being Companions

$\mathcal{G}$od has given you and your mate
different skills and responsibilities. Don't
constantly blame your mate for things that
are undone. Ask yourself, "Is some of this
MY responsibility?" Work together in
harmony and a spirit of companionship.

BLAME

*It is better to dwell in a corner of the housetop,
than with a brawling woman in a wide house.*
PROVERBS 21:9

Being Companions

*W*hat will you do to show your mate how much your love means? Let your beloved know you'd be willing to go to great lengths again if necessary. Then put your actions to work to win your mate all over again. Rekindle your love with a fresh, new commitment.

WINNING

And Jacob loved Rachel; and said, 'I will serve thee seven years for Rachel thy younger daughter.'
GENESIS 29:18

Being Companions

*W*hen metal strikes metal, both become more finely honed. The same is true with intelligence in two people. Challenge your beloved — and yourself — to greater mental thoughts. Read widely, understand broadly, push yourself to greater awareness of the world around you.

INTELLECT

Iron sharpeneth iron; so a man sharpeneth the countenance of his friend.
PROVERBS 27:17

Being Companions

*G*entleness is like oil that smooths the friction of day to day living. Gentleness inspires love and affection. Be extra gentle to your mate as you walk through your days together.

FRICTION

Let the husband render unto the wife due benevolence: and likewise also the wife unto the husband.
1 CORINTHIANS 7:3

Being Companions

*L*ove your mate with your whole body and soul. Luxuriate in the delights of your love. Romance blooms gently in the midst of tenderness and thoughtfulness. Enjoy the love you share.

WHOLENESS

From whom the whole body fitly joined together and...working in the measure of every part, maketh increase of the body unto edifying of itself in love.

EPHESIANS 4:16

Being Companions

$\mathscr{L}$ove molds you into many of the shapes and attitudes of your beloved. Seek to grow in positive ways with your mate. Decide together on what is important in the lives you share. You are two...but your hearts must beat as one.

LIKEMINDED

Fulfill ye my joy, that ye be likeminded, having the same love, being of one accord, of one mind.
PHILIPPIANS 2:2

145

Being Companions

*H*idden anger and bitterness can turn a love relationship into a cold war. Guard against undealt-with anger in your heart and learn to talk to your beloved about any hurts or disappointments that arise.

BITTERNESS

Wives, submit yourselves unto your own husbands, as it is fit in the Lord. Husbands, love your wives, and be not bitter against them.
COLOSSIANS 3:18,19

Being Companions

*T*he vows you took on your wedding day are the most life-changing promises you will ever make. Esteem and honor your vows. Never forsake the love that brought you together.

WEDDING VOWS

For this cause shall a man leave his father and mother, and shall be joined unto his wife, and they two shall be one flesh.
EPHESIANS 5:31

Being Companions

$\mathcal{G}$od's hand is the one that fashioned you and your beloved—your personalities, your intellects, your deepest desires. Rejoice in His presence in your life together and give Him your devotion.

DEVOTION

*Lord thou has been our dwelling place
in all generations.*

PSALM 90:1

Being Companions

*G*od has promised a dwelling place for you. When the difficulties of your life and your relationships seem dry and unfulfilling, come to the Lord who loves you for refreshment and renewed hope.

DWELLING

...Strong is thy dwellingplace and thou puttest thy nest in a rock.
NUMBERS 24:21

Being Companions

*T*he Father who led Moses out of the wilderness promises to lead you to a special promised land as well. Accept His guidance and follow His leading to a place overflowing with milk and honey.

INHERITANCE

The seed also of his servants shall inherit it: and they that love His name shall dwell therein,
PSALM 69:36

Being Companions

*A*rrogance can crush love quicker than almost anything. True love is built on acceptance and kindness one toward another. Protect your relationship with your beloved from the harshness of arrogance.

ARROGANCE

...Yea, all of you be subject one to another, and be clothed with humility: for God resisteth the proud, and giveth grace to the humble.

1 PETER 5:5b

Being Companions

*R*ejection can cut through love like a knife through fine cloth. If you feel rejected, take your hurt to God. He knows the wounds of the rejected and knows how to heal them.

REJECTION

But first must he suffer many things, and be rejected of this generation.
LUKE 17:25

Being Companions

*T*he very core of love is found in the heart of God. If your love has grown stale, ask God to give you an abundance of the love He so generously gives to those who ask of Him. It's still true...ASK and you shall RECEIVE. Accept His generous offer of love today for you and your beloved.

ABUNDANCE

*For in Him we live, and move,
and have our being;...*
ACTS 17:28a

153

Being Companions

A listening heart is a balm to a damaged relationship. Be willing to see your relationship through the eyes of your mate. God has given you ears to hear. Ask Him to help you listen wisely.

LISTEN

The hearing ear, and the seeing eye, the Lord hath made even both of them.
PROVERBS 20:12

Working Together

*T*he burdens of life may seem to be impossible. Every day you observe your own weaknesses and those of your beloved. Then you remember what brought you together in the first place. You recall that a couple in love can pull a heavier load together than each can pull alone. It's what commitment to "stick together" is all about.

COMMITMENT

Then shall the earth yield her increase; and God, even our own God, shall bless us.
PSALM 67:6

155

Working Together

*T*rue love is not easily embarrassed. Seek to help work out the plan God has for your beloved's life. Never allow the teasing or ridicule of others to ever stop you from being 100% supportive of your mate. Because when it's all said and done, all you really have on earth is each other.

SUPPORT

But Noah found grace in the eyes of the Lord...And the Lord said unto Noah, "Come thou and all thy house into the ark; for thee have I seen righteous before me in this generation."

GENESIS 6:8, 7:1

Working Together

*A*n enduring, loving marriage is a wondrous monument to the goodness of a gracious Lord. As your grey hairs begin to appear, and as your bodies start to slow down, let your love for each other increase. Your life together is your greatest work for God.

AGING

Now also when I am old and greyheaded, O God, forsake me not; until I have shewed thy strength unto this generation, and thy power to every one that is to come.

PSALM 71:18

Working Together

*T*hank God daily for the bountiful privileges He has given to you and your spouse. Consider what your marriage and family would be like if you did not have the freedoms you are able to enjoy together. Rejoice in God's blessings. Be thankful for your liberty today as you bring to mind our country's independence.

FREEDOM

His seed shall be mighty upon earth: the generation of the upright shall be blessed.
PSALM 112:2

Working Together

*L*ove isn't all hugs and laughter. Love that's deep and solid also involves hard work and sweat. Spend time working with your beloved. When it's tough, do it tough. When it's easy, do it easy. Then take the time to stand back together and enjoy the fruits of your labour together.

LABOUR

Two are better than one; because they have a good reward for their labour.
ECCLESIASTES 4:9

Working Together

*O*ur Almighty Father, Ruler of the heavens and King of all the earth, wants to bless you today. Gratefully accept His love and kind benediction as you and your beloved go about your daily tasks.

BENEDICTION

God be merciful unto us, and bless us; and cause His face to shine upon us; Selah.
PSALM 67:1

Working Together

*L*ive so you may look upon your work and pronounce it good. Let pride shine in your face when your labour is worthy of praise. Give glory to God for what He has enabled you and your beloved mate to accomplish.

PRIDE

Wherefore I perceive that there is nothing better, than that a man should rejoice in his own works; for that is his portion: for who shall bring him to see what shall be after him?
ECCLESIASTES 3:22

Working Together

*L*ove does not grow by iron-clad rules that seek to bend others to our own way. Love grows in the gentle breeze of acceptance. Love your mate closer to your heart with gentleness, not legislation.

RULES

Love worketh no ill to his neighbour: therefore love is the fulfilling of the law.
ROMANS 13:10

Working Together

*N*ot all work is done through strength. Some of the best and most enduring work is accomplished when two lovers are at the point of their greatest weakness, both spiritually and physically. Don't wait to be strong to do what God wants you to do. Simply put your hand to the task to be done *today*.

WEAKNESS

Blessed is the man whose strength is in thee: in whose heart are the ways of them.
PSALM 84:5

Working Together

*T*he best part of love is not in its intelligence. Love is notoriously blind. Nor does the best part lie in its unending hope. No, the best part of love is simply in its seeking the very best for your mate — and wanting that "best" for your beloved more than you desire it for yourself.

BEST

And though I have the gift of prophecy and understand all mysteries, and all knowledge; and though I have all faith, so that I could remove mountains, and have not charity, I am nothing.

1 CORINTHIANS 13:2

Working Together

*M*ake it a daily decision that you and your mate train your eyes to behold the workings of the Lord. Seek to see His Hand in the events around you. Then give outward thanks to Him for His help in the life of your family.

WORKINGS

I will meditate also of all thy work, and talk of thy doings.
PSALM 77:12

Working Together

*T*wo hearts don't always beat as one. However, in the important matters of your life together seek harmony with your mate so you can experience the joy of life with agreement and a deep sense of meaning and purpose.

ACCORD

Again I say unto you, That if two of you shall agree on earth as touching any thing that they shall ask, it shall be done for them of my Father which is in heaven.

MATTHEW 18:19

Working Together

*T*he desire to mate and build a family is given to people from a God who said "be fruitful, multiply, and fill the earth." It's vital you and your spouse regard your "child rearing years" as among the most fulfilling work of your entire lives. You are designing our world's future.

GENERATIONS

Thy seed will I establish for ever, and build up thy throne to all generations. Selah.
PSALM 89:4

Working Together

*L*ie down in repose in the warmth of God's love. His power protects you so you can frolic with your beloved. He smiles when He sees the love that flows between you and your mate in your most tender moments.

PROTECTION

For the Lord God is a sun and shield: the Lord will give grace and glory: no good thing will He withhold from them that walk uprightly.

PSALM 84:11

Working Together

*G*od doesn't stay home in the morning; He goes to work with you. Never forget that He is beside you with each decision and task you need to do during the business day. Ask Him for any wisdom you lack and He will give it to you from the abundance of a Father's heart.

SUBDUED

Is not the Lord your God with you? and hath he not given you rest on every side? For he hath given the inhabitants of the land into mine hand; and the land is subdued before the Lord, and before his people.

I CHRONICLES 22:18

Working Together

*G*od has made you and your mate as individuals. He gave each of you different talents and abilities. Ask Him how He would like you to use these gifts in His service. Always use your gifts to glorify the Lord!

INDIVIDUALS

Thy hands have made me and fashioned me: give me understanding, that I may learn thy commandments.
PSALM 119:73

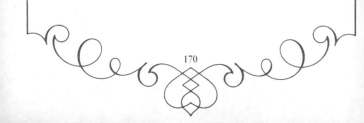

Working Together

*H*ow do you handle criticism? How do you respond to the inadequacies in yourself and others? Are you sensitive to the needs and ambitions of others? Let God teach you to reflect His love and understanding in the workplace.

RESPONSE

I therefore, the prisoner of the Lord, beseech you that ye walk worthy of the vocation wherewith ye are called, With all lowliness and meakness, with longsuffering, forbearing one another in love.

EPHESIANS 4:1,2

Working Together

*W*isdom from God makes the difference between a successful career and a series of failures. The Bible gives you and your mate a solid foundation for relating justly and honestly to those around you. Ask God for more wisdom to build a strong foundation as you work together to make your relationship a success.

CAREER

Teach me good judgment and knowledge: for I have believed thy commandments.
PSALM 119:66

Working Together

*L*ove is a golden thread that, when woven throughout your days, makes your life a beautiful tapestry for all to see. Don't ration the love you share with your mate. Give your love freely — with an almost reckless abandon. Let your love be a pleasant blend of all that is wonderful and good.

TAPESTRY

Rest in the Lord, and wait patiently for him...
PSALM 37:7a

Working Together

*M*ake a pact with your spouse to indulge yourselves with the love of God. God specializes in good gifts. The gift of your mate is but one example of God's boundless caring. He has given you a beloved one to love even as He has given Himself generously to you. Stretch your love and let it grow today.

STRETCH

Every good gift and every perfect gift is from above, and cometh down from the Father of lights, with whom is no variableness, neither shadow of turning.
JAMES 1:17

Working Together

*A*s you and your spouse engage in business, exercise caution in accepting counsel from those whose ethics may be in question. Pick your counselors and business associates with great care. Your reputation, integrity and honor is at stake.

ETHICS

Blessed is the man that walketh not in the counsel of the ungodly...And he shall be like a tree planted by the rivers of water, that bringeth forth his fruit in his season...

PSALM 1:1a,3a

Working Together

*G*od created you and your spouse as natural leaders. In your workplaces seek ways to demonstrate your leadership skills. Encourage growth in your mate in all areas of life. If you want to be a leader — LEAD! Others who value your guidance will follow — especially if you have children.

LEADERSHIP

...God created he him; male and female created he them. And God...said unto them, Be fruitful and multiply; and replenish the earth and subdue it: and have dominion over...every living thing that moveth upon the earth.

GENESIS 1:27b,28

Working Together

*H*onor God with the first place in
your affections. Give a worthy portion to
Him before you spend liberally on yourself.
Agree with your spouse to bring the fruits
of your work to God and give them to Him
with devotion.

TITHE

*Honour the Lord with thy substance, and with
the firstfruits of all thine increase: So shall thy
barns be filled with plenty, and thy presses shall
burst out with new wine.*

PROVERBS 3:9,10

Working Together

*W*hen seeking an occupation,
follow your natural abilities and desires.
God has given you and your beloved skills
unmatched by others. He wants you to use
them to His glory. Work diligently as unto
the Lord and He will bless your labour.

OCCUPATION

Delight thyself also in the Lord, And He shall give
thee the desires of thine heart.
PSALM 37:4

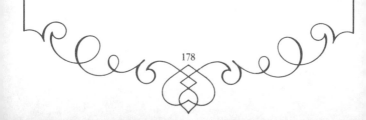

Working Together

*I*t can be wearisome to feel all alone in one's work, especially when the burdens are heavy. A responsive God saw the loneliness in man's heart and made for him a friend, a companion, a wife. Enjoy each other to the fullest. Do something extra special for each other today.

WIFE

And the Lord God said, It is not good that the man should be alone: I will make him an help meet for him.
GENESIS 2:18

Working Together

$\int$ ome of the most challenging labour in life takes place in the home. It's difficult to be a parent without having someone else to help you in the hard times. Lean on your spouse for support in raising your children.

PARENTING

For if they fall, one will lift up his fellow: but woe to him that is alone when he falleth, for he hath not another to help him up.

ECCLESIASTES 4:10

Working Together

$\mathcal{G}$od has set a standard for you and your spouse. Honesty and integrity are among the two most important yardsticks He has created to measure your performance. Is there anything that needs improvement? Talk it over. Listen to each other. If need be make some changes. Start today.

YARDSTICK

For the word of the Lord is right; and all His works are done in truth.

PSALM 33:4

Working Together

$\mathcal{L}$et God's abundance and love flow through you and your beloved. God is a generous rewarder to those who show mercy and kindness to others. Find someone needy to love. Reach out beyond yourselves in practical kindness.

PRACTICAL

And when ye reap the harvest of your land, thou shalt not wholly reap the corners of thy field, neither shalt thou gather the gleanings of thy harvest.
LEVITICUS 19:9

Working Together

*A*lways give your beloved verbal credit for a job well done. Know that God rewards His children who honestly and righteously serve Him in the workplace. Encourage yourself and your mate through the difficult times. Be sure to go out of your way to give credit where it's due.

CREDIT

Seest thou a man diligent in his business? He shall stand before kings; he shall not stand before mean men.
PROVERBS 22:29

Working Together

*T*he Lord gives and the Lord takes away. God is the one who controls your destiny and your days. If you or your beloved lack anything, go to the Heavenly Father and ask Him. He is pleased to provide for His children.

PROVIDER

And he said unto them, Cast the net on the right side of the ship, and ye shall find. They cast therefore, and now they were not able to draw it for the multitude of fishes.

JOHN 21:6

Being Known

*Y*our soul cries out to be known by
someone special. And even as
you are drawn to a deeper, more intimate
relationship with your mate, a loving God
chooses to draw you both closer to
Himself. Your heavenly Father wants to
be known, loved and served. Live in the
comfort of knowing your Father cares.

KNOWN

*But as for me, my prayer is unto thee, O Lord,
in an acceptable time: O God, in the multitude
of thy mercy hear me, in the truth
of thy salvation.*
PSALM 69:13

Being Known

*D*elight in searching out the hidden places of your beloved's mind and soul. Love the dark, shadowy places and rejoice where there is light in abundance. Give your heart to your own love and none other. Leave room for hidden mysteries.

HIDDEN

Drink waters out of thine own cistern, and running waters out of thine own well.
PROVERBS 5:15

Being Known

*S*ing softly of your beloved's virtues.
Praise all good things. Let your pride be
seen on your face. Let your love for your
spouse be a hiding place for your
beloved's imperfections.

IMPERFECTIONS

*And above all these things put on charity, which
is the bond of perfectness.*
COLOSSIANS 3:14

Being Known

*A*fter the sun has set and darkness covers your face, seek the sweet communion of time spent with your beloved at the merciful Throne of our Father. He will give you comfort in times of trial and sustenance when the challenges seem too great. Believe in His great mercy today.

EVENING

I call to remembrance my song in the night: I commune with mine own heart: and my spirit made diligent search.

PSALM 77:6

Being Known

*G*aze upon the sleeping face of your beloved. When you were courting, words were not enough to describe your mate's inner and outer beauty. Still, you want to know your beloved in greater depth. Keep the exploration alive today and every day. Never be satisfied. Always know there is more to be discovered about your beloved.

SEARCHING

The spirit of man is the candle of the LORD, searching all the inward parts of the belly.
PROVERBS 20:27

Being Known

*T*o some, love comes in a whisper.
For others, it arrives with a great
tumultuous shout! But from the beginning,
words were important. Words either build
or destroy. Let your positive, loving speech
— coupled with "love actions" — be the
proof of your love.

SPEECH

*Let your speech be alway with grace, seasoned
with salt, that ye may know how ye ought
to answer every man.*
COLOSSIANS 4:6

Being Known

Loving criticism is better than lying praise. The one purifies so wounds can heal. The other encourages infection so that a temporary peace can be maintained. Speak the truth in love with your mate. Do not shy away from caring, honest reproof.

CRITICISM

Faithful are the wounds of a friend; but the kisses of an enemy are deceitful.
PROVERBS 27:6

Being Known

*W*edding days are rapturous and exciting. Congratulations and happy tears abound. But the wedding day ecstasy cannot endure forever. Each 24 hours has its own texture. Appreciate each day for its own value. Like a game of chess, no game — or day — is ever the same. Enjoy the difference. Appreciate the variety of your love.

APPRECIATE

Say not thou, 'What is the cause that the former days were better than these?' for thou dost not inquire wisely concerning this.

ECCLESIASTES 7:10

Being Known

*T*rue politeness is grounded in considerate truth. When seeking to know your beloved, don't be content with anything less than straightforward, honest communication. The roots of true love grow deeply when the truth is spoken with compassion and love.

POLITENESS

Keep thy tongue from evil, and thy lips from speaking guile.
PSALM 34:13

Being Known

*L*ook at the face of your beloved and you will see flashes of gold. But, in fact, what you see is much more precious than gold. A love rooted and grounded in God makes your lover's countenance shine more than any earthly treasures.

TREASURE

For where your treasure is, there will your heart be also.
LUKE 12:34

Being Known

A love that refuses to show its face is a worthless love. Without action and light, love becomes twisted and withered. Love needs acknowledgement to grow to full force. Let the light of God's love shine on you and your mate today and every day as you continue to stand together in love.

LIGHT

Open rebuke is better than secret love.
PROVERBS 27:5

Being Known

*H*ate and love are flip sides of the same coin. And sometimes only a coin's width separates the two. Love can be wounded so severely that it can lose its value, and can deteriorate into hate and despair. Make both sides of your coin read "I love you." *Heads you win... tails you win too!*

HATE

Howbeit he would not hearken unto her voice: but, being stronger than she, forced her, and lay with her. Then Amnon hated her exceedingly; so that the hatred wherewith he hated her was greater than the love wherewith he had loved her...

II SAMUEL 13:14,15a

Being Known

L ove is much like an orchestra responding to the skill and care of a conductor. No single instrument can ever be the sole star. The music and the harmony of all players working together is what makes the place a thing of beauty. Live in that kind of harmony with your spouse. If there is discord in your heart, "conduct it out" today.

HARMONY

Charity...Doth not behave itself unseemly, seeketh not her own, is not easily provoked, thinketh no evil.
1 CORINTHIANS 13:4a,5

Being Known

*Y*ou married because you "fell in love." Now as your love matures you find yourself "standing in love" — an even more mature form of affection. When you truly love you ask, "What can I do for you?" not "What are you going to do for me?" Love is an "inside job"...but once it emerges, the outward expression of your affection makes a world of difference to your beloved.

MARRIED

So ought men to love their wives as their own bodies. He that loveth his wife loveth himself.
EPHESIANS 5:28

Being Known

*P*riceless pearls are created in the deep, hidden recesses of the oyster shell. Let your heart and soul be as one of those pearls of great price — quietly growing in value every day. Start living this way today!

PEARLS

Whose adorning let it not be that outward adorning...But let it be the hidden man of the heart, in that which is not corruptible, even the ornament of a meek and quiet spirit, which is in the sight of God of great price.

I PETER 3:3a,4

Being Known

*Y*our love can be a quiet, flickering candle or a roaring fire. But your true love has flame *only because God has given you the enormous capacity to love.* Thank God for the ability He has freely given to you to share your deepest affection with your beloved.

FLAME

Beloved, let us love one another: for love is of God; and every one that loveth is born of God, and knoweth God.

I JOHN 4:7

Being Known

*D*oes your love harbor fears? Will your beloved still love you if your secrets are known? Love and acceptance grow only in the light of the truth. When you finally share a deep secret with your mate, do it with love and care. Shame can turn to joy when you speak the truth in love.

SHAME

But speaking the truth in love, may grow up into him in all things, which is the head, even Christ.

EPHESIANS 4:15

Being Known

*L*ove is the light that guides you in your relationship with your beloved. But your love isn't perfect. Never has been and never will. Love can stumble and cause pain. All that is required is for you to put the good of your beloved ahead of your own desires. If you stumble, pick yourself up and start all over again.

STUMBLING

He that loveth his brother abideth in the light, and there is none occasion of stumbling in him.
I JOHN 2:10

Being Known

*N*ot all of the ways of the Lord are plain to our earthly eyes. Sometimes the workings of the Father are subtle and can only be observed by the most discerning mind. Seek to know how God is working in the lives of you and your beloved.

DISCERNMENT

The secret of the LORD is with them that fear him, and he will show them his covenant.
PSALM 25:14

Being Known

*L*ove makes mistakes. But a willingness to set things right is more important to your beloved than feigned perfection. Don't pretend when you don't know what to do in your relationship. Talk with your beloved. Two-way communication unearths hidden treasure.

PRETENSE

Who can understand his errors? Cleanse thou me from secret faults.
PSALM 19:12

Being Known

*W*hen you share from the center of your heart, you give a gift beyond value to your beloved. Take time to give this greatest of all treasures to your spouse. Share your personal secrets with your lover alone. True intimacy will be your reward.

INTIMACY

And Adam knew his wife again; and she bare a son, and called his name Seth...

GENESIS 4:25a

Being Known

*C*ourage is the tool that sculpts and refines a loving marriage. It takes courage to tell your beloved that you have been hurt by words or deeds. But do not neglect the cleansing of your hurt feelings. If you do, they will fester and injure your love. Have the courage to speak of your feelings...and do it with love in your heart.

COURAGE

Moreover if thy brother shall trespass against thee, go and tell him his fault between thee and him alone...
MATTHEW 18:15a

Being Known

*C*ompliments are like a welcome summer breeze after the gales of winter. Tell your beloved of the beauty your eyes see. Speak often of your deep, deep love and your relationship will blossom. It's still true...you will always reap what you sow. Speak love and you harvest love. Let your marriage be a trophy of caring.

BEAUTY

As the lily among thorns, so is my love among the daughters.
SONG OF SOLOMON 2:2

Being Known

*O*ur Father in heaven has given you and your beloved a bountiful marriage. Feast on the delights of your love for each other. Rejoice in the sensations of being joined to your beloved. Feel your love to the edges and live in the exhilaration of your affection.

SENSATIONS

And they were both naked, the man and his wife, and were not ashamed.
GENESIS 2:25

Being Known

*T*he health of your marriage rests on the mercy of a loving, living God. He is the One who can make the rough ways smooth and heal your broken heart. He steadfastly gives strength to you — His child. He is generous, loving and kind. Rely on His grace to keep your marriage healthy and strong.

GIRDETH

It is God that girdeth me with strength, and maketh my way perfect.
PSALM 18:32

Being Known

*T*rue love is spun with the purest of golden thoughts. You dream enchanted dreams of the next time you will be alone with your mate. Strangely and beautifully, time both slows down and speeds up when you are in the presence of your beloved. Keep your love alive in a fresh, creative way. Recapture the wonder of your love.

ENCHANTMENT

And Jacob served seven years for Rachel; and they seemed unto him but a few days, for the love he had to her.

GENESIS 29:20

Being Known

*Y*ou look into the face of your beloved, searching for a sign of romantic devotion, for a quickly returned glance of adoration. Then you see it in your beloved's eyes — you are well loved. You embrace. You have rediscovered why you are standing in love.

LOOKING

And when Boaz had eaten and drunk, and his heart was merry, he went to lie down at the end of the heap of corn: and she came softly, and uncovered his feet, and laid her down.

RUTH 3:7

Being Known

*W*rap yourself in God's holiness. He wants to be your hiding place when you feel sad and forsaken by those who say they love you. He is waiting to comfort and encourage you every day. He will never leave you nor forsake you. That's His promise to you!

FORSAKEN

But thou, O LORD, art a shield for me; my glory, and the lifter up of mine head.
PSALM 3:3

Being Known

*Y*our love relationship is a place for you to know your emotions, own your emotions and show your emotions. Your fears, joys, concerns, hurts and sky-splitting moments of ecstasy are all a part of the person God made you to be. Celebrate them all with your beloved.

EMOTIONS

From the end of the earth will I cry unto thee, when my heart is overwhelmed: lead me to the rock that is higher than I.
PSALM 61:2

Being Known

*P*romises broken and promises kept — these two things both build and destroy trust. Let your words come from your mouth as words that come from your heart. Promise your beloved only what you feel you can deliver.

PROMISES

For thou, O God, hast heard my vows...
PSALM 61:5a

Being Known

*C*omfort is the backbone of love. Accept your beloved for who he is. Don't over-correct your spouse with words of torment or reproof. Learn instead to stand beside your beloved with quiet encouragement. If you need to begin this new behavior, start doing it today.

CORRECTION

I have heard many such things:
miserable comforters are ye all.
JOB 16:2

Living With Hope

*L*ift your eyes to the Lord of the Heavens and ask Him to shower your love relationship with grace. He is the One who enables you to love. It is He who gives you more ability to love if you ask Him. May His love encompass you and your beloved today.

SHOWERS

He shall come down like rain upon the mown grass: as showers that water the earth.

PSALM 72:6

Living With Hope

*D*rink your fill of the kisses of your beloved. Savour the warmth of your lover's closeness. God smiles to see the love you share with your mate. Rejoice in your life together.

KISSES

Let him kiss me with the kisses of his mouth:
for thy love is better than wine.
SONG OF SOLOMON 1:2

Living With Hope

$\mathcal{W}$hen enemies are camped around you and your beloved, do not fear. The God who reigns over all the earth and heavens will be your defender and will shield you from harm.

SHIELD

Behold, O God our shield, and look upon the face of thine anointed.
PSALM 84:9

Living With Hope

*L*oving someone is not always easy. Everyone has blocks that often stand in the way. Too many times old hurts make us cautious in love. Ask God to continue to bring you to maturity and give you the capacity to love as never before.

CAPACITY

Being confident of this very thing, that he which hath begun a good work in you will perform it until the day of Jesus Christ.

PHILIPPIANS 1.6

Living With Hope

*C*enter your heart around God and He will give you the desires of your heart. Come to God with your mate and dedicate your love to Him. Thank Him for giving you your life's companion.

CENTER

Rejoice the soul of thy servant: for unto thee, O Lord do I lift up my soul.

PSALM 86:4

Living With Hope

*L*ove your mate with confidence. Support your beloved's strengths while not shying away from the weaknesses. They are all part of being human. Believe the best of your mate even as you accept the frailness of your beloved.

ACCEPTANCE

Charity...Beareth all things, believeth all things, hopeth all things, endureth all things.
1 CORINTHIANS 13:4a,7

Living With Hope

*D*ance with your love before the Lord. Be merry in your affection as you serenade each other with laughter. Feel the warm smile of God upon the lives of you and your beloved. Celebrate your togetherness...NOW!

MERRY

Glory ye in his holy name: let the heart of them rejoice that seek the Lord.
PSALM 105:3

Living With Hope

 $\mathscr{G}$ ive the precious gift of your heart to God first and then to your beloved. Do not hold back. Give of yourself freely without counting the price. You'll be rewarded over and over for your efforts.

PRECIOUS

There came unto him a woman having an alabaster box of very precious ointment, and poured it on his head, as he sat at meat.
MATTHEW 26:7

Living With Hope

*L*ove ebbs and flows. If you are feeling low on affection, ask God to renew the melody of love that once sang in your heart. God is the God of new beginnings. He will give you all you ask of Him.

RENEWAL

Thou sendest forth thy spirit, they are created: and thou renewest the face of the earth.
PSALM 104:30

Living With Hope

*L*et gladness surround your love and lighten the hearts of all who see the devotion you share with your mate. Treat your beloved like the priceless treasure that God has shaped and designed for you.

GLADNESS

And he brought forth his people with joy, and his chosen with gladness.

PSALM 105:43

Living With Hope

A loving heart binds up hurts with a patient and forgiving spirit. When you or your beloved stumble, don't give up walking toward each other. Everyone makes mistakes in love. Remember often what drew you together in the first place. Have patience and rediscover each other as the bond you share strengthens daily.

PATIENCE

And the Lord direct your hearts into the love of God, and into the patient waiting for Christ.
II THESSALONIANS 3:5

Living With Hope

$\mathcal{G}$od spoke the world into being. His voice rang out throughout the universe and all that lived leapt to obey His command. Ask God to speak in your life with your beloved. Let His love and wisdom be yours in all your dealings this day and always.

VOICE

The voice of the Lord maketh the hinds to calve, and discovereth the forests: and in his temple doth every one speak of his glory.
PSALM 29:9

Living With Hope

*T*ime belongs to God. Ask Him to make you a wise steward of the 24-hours each day He has given you. Spend time with your spouse and speak frankly and openly about the concerns of your heart. Always make time for each other.

TIME

And the Lord appointed a set time, saying Tomorrow the Lord shall do this thing in the land.
EXODUS 9:5

Living With Hope

*M*arriage is a great teacher. You see your own faults more clearly when placed up against another's needs. Thank God for His help as you grow into the person He wants you to be. Life is your school, and your mate is one of your best teachers. Learn well today and everyday.

LEARNING

Now unto him that is able to keep you from falling, and to present you faultless before the presence of his glory with exceeding joy.
JUDE 24

Living With Hope

 $\mathcal{G}$ od leads you into pleasant pastures.
Ask Him to bring you and your beloved to
a quiet oasis where He may give you a time
of rest in your life together. Focus on your
beloved and confess all the love that has
grown in your heart thus far.

PLEASANTNESS

*So we thy people and sheep of thy pasture will
give thee thanks for ever: we will shew forth
thy praise to all generations.*
PSALM 79:13

Living With Hope

*W*hen people receive a great gift, they usually cannot wait to tell everyone they know about it. Your mate is one of God's greatest blessings to you. Make sure other people know of your regard for your beloved. Don't keep your beloved's good qualities a secret. Speak of your blessings to others.

BLESSINGS

And all nations shall call you blessed: for ye shall be a delightsome land, saith the Lord of Hosts.
MALACHI 3:12

Living With Hope

*L*ove liberates. It can give you both wings to fly and a place to stand. Seek to give your mate courage and the space to grow into all that God has designed. Live a life of love and it will set you free.

LIBERATION

And I will walk at liberty: for I seek thy precepts.
PSALM 119:45

Living With Hope

*L*ife can seem like a series of closed doors. Don't be afraid to ask to have the doors opened. God wants you and your beloved to seek what you want and you will find it. That is His generous promise to you.

SEEKING

The heart of the prudent getteth Knowledge; and the ear of the wise seeketh Knowledge.

PROVERBS 18:15

Living With Hope

*F*ocus your heart on the heart of God and He will work miracles in your love life. Seek to follow God's example as you relate to your loved one. He will bless you as your minds and hearts are stayed on Him.

FOCUS

O God, my heart is fixed; I will sing and give praise, even with my glory.
PSALM 108:1

Living With Hope

*L*et your mind savour sweetness, whether it is a sweet thought of your beloved or a sweet moment with the Lord. Soak your being in love and let affection be the hallmark that describes your life.

SWEETNESS

The wise in heart shall be called prudent: and the sweetness of the lips increaseth learning.
PROBERBS 16:21

Living With Hope

*W*hen you truly love and are loved by someone, there is little need for secrets. After all, most of your faults and shortcomings are already known to the other. The good news is that those in love *accept each other anyway.*

REVEALING

He revealeth the deep and secret things: he knoweth what is in the darkness, and the light dwelleth with Him.
DANIEL 2:22

Living With Hope

*G*od is the surgeon who sees the wounds — large or small — in our spirits and can make them well. He sees what we seek to hide and He knows the worth of our love for others. Let God today be the surgeon in your lives. Let Him do whatever is necessary to make you whole.

WEIGHS

All the ways of a man are clean in his own eyes; but the Lord weigheth the spirits.

PROVERBS 16:2

Living With Hope

*I*f inner troubles plague your marriage, don't give up. The One who has borne all your transgressions is also the One who gives you hope for a new tomorrow. He walks with you and your mate. He will never leave you or leave you comfortless. That's His promise to you. Believe it. Live your life *knowing it is true.*

TRANSGRESSIONS

Surely he hath borne our griefs, and carried our sorrows: yet we did esteem him stricken, smitten of God, and afflicted.
ISAIAH 53:4

Living With Hope

$\mathcal{T}$hink about our Lord's birth in a manger. Sing praises to God for the wondrous way in which He showed His endless love to all of mankind. Be thankful for the gift of a mate who loves and cares about this priceless gift.

GLORY

Glory to God in the highest and on earth peace, good will toward man.

LUKE 2:14

Living With Hope

*R*eflect on the miracle of Jesus' birth and ask Him to continue the miracle of love He has begun inside of you. Renew your vows with your mate. Let this day be one of joy, fulfillment and hope.

MIRACLE

And thou shalt have joy and gladness; and many shall rejoice at his birth.
LUKE 1:14

Living With Hope

Despair is only for a span of time. God can bring your heart to a place of rejoicing and gladness. Thank Him for the care He gives to all of His children. The four most comforting words in the English language are: *This too shall pass.* Don't despair...joy comes in the morning.

DESPAIR

O satisfy us early with thy mercy; that we may rejoice and be glad all our days.
PSALM 90:14

Living With Hope

*L*ove bursts forth from your heart
and waters the days of your beloved. You
scarcely feel the love leaving you. Then you
see the result. Love brings forth
life in barren wastelands.

LIFE

Let thy fountains be dispersed abroad,
and rivers of waters in the streets.
PROVERBS 5:16

Living With Hope

$\mathcal{M}$ake of your love a safe sanctuary for you and your beloved. Keep your relationship with your mate healthy and strong so it may be a place of comfort and retreat from the troubles of life.

SANCTUARY

And he brought them to the border of his sanctuary...
PSALM 78:54a

Living With Hope

*D*o not conform to the image of the world in your marriage. Spend time in God's Word and learn to love as God has loved. Be patient with your spouse and nurture your mate as God would. See that your values reflect those of the Father.

IMAGE

And be not conformed to this world: but be ye transformed by the renewing of your mind, that ye may prove what is that good, and acceptable, and perfect, will of God.
ROMANS 12:2

Living With Hope

*H*ope is a defense against many troubles in your life. Exercise hope as you talk with your mate. Pray in faith believing God will answer your prayers. Ground your hope in His love.

HOPE

Remember the word unto thy servant, upon which thou hast caused me to hope.
PSALM 119:49

Living With Hope

*C*onsider the ways in which God has
guided you and blessed your family. Pray
with your beloved for God to direct your
path each day of the year. May God grant to
you and your mate His very best this
day and every day to come.

CONSIDER

*I thought on my ways...At midnight I will rise to
give thanks unto thee because of
Thy righteous judgments.*
PSALM 119:59a,62

Facing Hard Times

$\mathcal{L}$ ove is a fortress against troubles from all sides. It will withstand fierce storms if your relationship is sturdy and strong. Be strong together.

FORTRESS

Better is a dinner of herbs where love is, than a stalled ox and hatred therewith.
PROVERBS 15:17

Facing Hard Times

*D*evelop a sense of oneness with your partner. Use disagreements to build your relationship by talking about problems when they occur. Don't let resentment build a wall between you. If you do, it can become a wedge that can split you apart.

ONENESS

And if a house be divided against itself, that house cannot stand.

MARK 3:25

Facing Hard Times

*I*f you feel overwhelmed by the storms in your relationship with your beloved, don't despair. Ask God to come into the midst of your problems and bring you His calm and all abiding peace to strengthen your togetherness.

CALM

And he saith unto them, Why are ye fearful, O ye of little faith? Then he arose, and rebuked the winds and the sea; and there was a great calm.

MATTHEW 8:26

Facing Hard Times

*G*ive to your beloved until the cup
runs over. Don't wait to get from your loved
one before *you* show your love. When your
beloved is disappointed by life and its
cares, give your lover even more
love and support.

RUNS OVER

*But unto Hannah he gave a worthy portion;
for he loved Hannah: but the Lord
had shut up her womb.*
I SAMUEL 1:5

Facing Hard Times

*M*ake sure your actions match your words. Don't tell someone "I love you, oh, how I love you," and then neglect to show them love in action and deed. Be kind and considerate with your loved one.

CONSIDERATION

Though I speak with the tongues of men and of angels, and have not charity, I am become as sounding brass, or a tinkling cymbal.
I CORINTHIANS 13:1

Facing Hard Times

*C*ommit yourself to the promises of God in the hard times. Don't give way to a bottomless pit of despair. Talk to God about your feelings. Remind Him of the promises He has made to His people — to YOU!

COMMIT

Blessed is the man that endureth temptation: for when he is tried, he shall receive the crown of life, which the Lord hath promised to them that love Him.

JAMES 1:12

Facing Hard Times

$\mathcal{D}$on't underestimate the power of love to see you through the hard times. Faith and hope are vital. But the Bible tells us that love continues to win the day. Tell your mate of your love even more when the hard times come.

CHARITY

And now abideth faith, hope, charity, these three; but the greatest of these is charity.
1 CORINTHIANS 13:13

Facing Hard Times

*B*e grateful for these times with your mate that are filled with richness, quietness and contentment. Don't let the pursuit of money or fame become a substitute for spending time nourishing your love relationship.

QUIETNESS

...In returning and rest shall ye be saved; in quietness and in confidence shall be your strength...
ISAIAH 30:15

Facing Hard Times

*L*ook for times in your love relationship when you can speak a word of encouragement or praise. Don't hesitate to tell of the joy you share with your loved one. Positive words strengthen the bond of love you share.

POSITIVE

A man hath joy by the answer of his mouth: and a word spoken in due season, how good is it!
PROVERBS 15:23

Facing Hard Times

*D*on't be misled. Adultery can never be hidden. The effects show in your life and your mate will know of your betrayal, even if it's only in the guilt you are trying to hide.

FIRE

Can a man take fire in his bosom, and his clothes not be burned?...So he that goeth in to his neighbor's wife; whosoever toucheth her shall not be innocent.

PROVERBS 6:27,29

Facing Hard Times

*R*emember, you don't have to face
your troubles alone. God is on the side of
His children and He will stand with you as
you face the obstacles in your life. Nor are
you alone in your physical relationship.
Stand strong with your beloved.

ENEMIES

*Through God we shall do valiantly: for he it
is that shall tread down our enemies.*
PSALM 108:13

Facing Hard Times

$\int$eek to find peace in the troubles and challenges of your relationship. Remember, love is not a contest, it is an exciting, cooperative venture that explores the uncharted worlds of relationship. Blessed is the one who makes peace.

STRIFE

It is an honour for a man to cease from strife: but every fool will be meddling.
PROVERBS 20:3

Facing Hard Times

*B*e careful about having too many secrets from your mate. Learn to be open and vulnerable. Openness develops trust and trust builds love. Ask God for courage to be *transparently YOU* with the one you love.

SECRETS

Stolen waters are sweet, and bread eaten in secret is pleasant. But he knoweth not that the dead are there; and that her guests are in the depths of hell.
PROVERBS 9:17,18

Facing Hard Times

*C*ome to God boldly. Ask Him what
you need to have in your relationship with
your beloved. The path of love will at times
be rough indeed. Ask God to help you
smooth the way. All you have to do is ask.

BOLDLY

Let us therefore come boldly unto the throne of
grace, that we may obtain mercy, and find
grace to help in time of need.
HEBREWS 4:16

Facing Hard Times

*B*eing angry is not a sin. However, be careful that your anger does not lead you to sin. Talk about your fears, frustrations and hurts with your beloved. Don't hold your anger inside.

FRUSTRATION

Be ye angry, and sin not; let not the sun go down upon your wrath.
EPHESIANS 4:26

Facing Hard Times

$\mathcal{T}$rue love outlasts the most difficult of times. Nourish your love in the hard times. It will make your troubles more bearable. Learn to stand close to your beloved when storms shake your household.

TENDERNESS

Charity never faileth: but whether there be prophecies, they shall fail; whether there be tongues, they shall cease; whether there be knowledge, it shall vanish away.

I CORINTHIANS 13:8

Facing Hard Times

$\mathcal{G}$od replaces your losses with good things. If you are following Him and lose someone close to you, always remember how much He cares, and that He's promised to fill your aching void with His special kind of love.

LOSSES

And Jesus answered and said, Verily I say unto you, There is no man that hath left house, or brethren, or sisters, or father, or mother, or wife, or children, or lands, for my sake, and the gospel's, But he shall receive an hundredfold now in this time...
MARK 10:29,30a

Facing Hard Times

*T*rue love doesn't just happen. It's God who gives us the power to love. If you find it difficult to express love, ask God for His direction and insight. He will give you the ability and the wisdom to love better and stronger than you ever dreamed possible.

WISE ONE

He that loveth not knoweth not God;
for God is love.
I JOHN 4:8

Facing Hard Times

*D*on't be misled. If you commit adultery you are doing more than just harming the relationship you share with your mate. You are doing what may be irreparable damage to your very soul. The guilt and deceit can eat away at your conscience until you are consumed.

DESTRUCTION

But whoso committeth adultery with a woman lacketh understanding: he that doeth it destroyeth his own soul.
PROVERBS 6:32

Facing Hard Times

*L*earn to be joyful and relish the love that you have with your mate. Don't let troubles rob you of an exuberant happiness in being together. Hug your lover and talk of your special feelings. Do it right now! Do it often!

RELISH

Live joyfully with the wife whom thou lovest...
ECCLESIASTES 9:9a

Facing Hard Times

*W*hen it seems like your troubles beat against you relentlessly, remember God
has promised to be your shade. He has promised to refresh you in the battles you face and to keep you.

SHADE

The Lord is thy keeper; the Lord is thy shade upon thy right hand.
PSALM 121:5

267

Facing Hard Times

*I*f you have problems, don't wait to take them to God. You can not face your hard times alone. Ask God to intervene and give you wisdom. He will stand with you in each situation. Better yet, together — you and your mate — take your problems and concerns to the Lord in earnest prayer.

ALONE

They wandered in the wilderness in a solitary way;...Then they cried unto the Lord in their trouble, and he delivered them out of their distresses.

PSALM 107:4a,6

Facing Hard Times

*I*f you and your mate are afraid and nervous, remember God has promised to send His angels and His Holy Spirit to watch over you. Do not worry, God is in charge and He loves you both more than you'll ever know.

NERVOUS

For He shall give His angels charge over thee,
to keep thee in all thy ways.
PSALM 91:11

Facing Hard Times

$\mathcal{G}$od specializes in new beginnings for couples. In the historic past as much as in the present, God has given new dreams to couples and has stood with them as their most cherished dreams came true. Don't be afraid to ask God for a new plan for your future.

DREAMS

And God said unto Abraham, "As for Sarai thy wife, thou shalt not call her name Sarai, but Sarah shall her name be. And I will bless her and give thee a son also of her: yea, I will bless her, and she shall be a mother of nations; kings of people shall be of her."
GENESIS 17:15,16

Facing Hard Times

*D*on't be a martyr to your mate.
Give from a joyful heart and not as one
who is forced to make sacrifices.
Remember true, abiding love comes from
the heart, not from the bank account.

SACRIFICES

*Better is a dry morsel, and quietness therewith,
than an house full of sacrifices with strife.*
PROVERBS 17:1

Facing Hard Times

*I*f it's been a while since you and your mate have turned to God and really listened to Him, don't despair. It's never too late for the repentant heart to seek His face. Do it together. Call on Him today.

RETURNING

Turn us again, O God, and cause thy face to shine; and we shall be saved.

PSALM 80:3

Facing Hard Times

$\mathcal{W}$hen you and your mate come before God, don't pretend you are satisfied when you are not. Talk over any misunderstandings you may have with one another. God longs for an honesty from His people who want to get to know Him more completely.

HONESTY

For he satisfieth the longing soul, and filleth the hungry soul with goodness.
PSALM 107:9

Facing Hard Times

*W*hen you are facing hard times,
don't worry if you seem to be weak and
helpless. God promises to give you His
strength to do what you need to do. Pray to
your loving Father and ask Him to bring
strength to your weakness.

STRENGTH

I will go in the strength of the Lord God:
I will make mention of thy righteousness,
even of thine only.
PSALM 71:16

Facing Hard Times

*W*hen you grieve, it's alright to weep. But don't weep as those couples who have no hope. The God of all creation listens to you when you mourn and He has promised to comfort you and bless you with good things.

GRIEF

He that goeth forth and weepeth, bearing precious seed, shall doubtless come again with rejoicing, bringing his sheaves with him.
PSALM 126:6

Growing With God

$\mathcal{G}$o to bed tonight with blissful thoughts of what God has done and is doing in your marriage and in your family life. Give thanks to Him and to your spouse for the happiness you are enjoying each day. Praise Him for your love together.

BLISSFUL

...The words of the pure are pleasant words.
PROVERBS 15:26

Growing With God

*I*f you are impatient with God's working in your love relationship, don't hesitate to tell Him the concerns of your heart. Right now, tell God you want a relationship that is meaningful and fulfilling for both you and your spouse. Ask the Lord to give you the wisdom to help you do *your* part to make your love stronger each day.

CHANGES

It is time for thee, Lord to work:
for they have made void thy law.
PSALM 119:126

Growing With God

*H*onesty is one of the most vital ingredients to a loving relationship. If you are afraid of being fully known by your beloved, practice by first being vulnerable before God. Share deeply with Him. Tell Him things unknown to others. Once you feel His boundless acceptance, you'll find yourself better prepared to be honest with your beloved.

VULNERABLE

*Search me, O God, and know my heart:
try me, and know my thoughts.*
PSALM 139:23

Growing With God

*W*hen you feel hurt or unloved, you may want to hit back. In your heart, you know that revenge doesn't build love. Talk about your hurts and disappointments with your beloved. Love your spouse today as never before.

REVENGE

Dearly beloved, avenge not yourselves, but rather give place unto wrath: for it is written, Vengeance is mine: I will repay, saith the Lord.

ROMANS 12:19

Growing With God

*D*oes your beloved seem far away, lost in concerns and problems? Everyone feels alone at times — uncared for and seemingly without a friend. Remember, that's one of the best times to draw nigh to God. Literally *see yourself cuddling in His arms.* He is your friend and constant companion. Then, take that spirit of God's love and share it with your mate. Enjoy an evening of cuddling...
of just being together.

CUDDLE

Draw nigh to God, and He will draw nigh to you.
JAMES 4:8a

Growing With God

*S*et aside a regular time to read God's Word with your beloved. As your souls grow closer to the soul of God, you will find yourselves growing closer to each other. Make *shared devotions* once a day a vital part of your relationship and your spiritual growth together.

DEVOTIONS

Search the scriptures; for in them ye think ye have eternal life; and they are they which testify of me.
JOHN 5:39

Growing With God

*R*ejoice in the pleasures God has given to you in your marriage. Thank Him for the abundance of affection and passion with which He has blessed you. Remember how He smiles when you drink deeply of His gifts.

PLEASURES

They shall be abundantly satisfied with the fatness of thy house; and thou shalt make them drink of the river of thy pleasures.

PSALM 36:8

Growing With God

*I*f you wish you had greater comprehension of your beloved, yourself and others, don't despair. God has promised His boundless wisdom to those who come to Him in faith — believing. Ask God to open your eyes. In so doing, you'll be like the blind man in the Bible who simply said, "Once I was blind, but now I can see." Ask God for that sight — and insight — today.

COMPREHENSION

Open thou mine eyes, that I may behold wondrous things out of thy law.
PSALM 119:18

Growing With God

*K*eep your eyes focussed on the positive, good things in your love relationship — the qualities that brought you together in the first place. Look for ways to compliment your beloved. A single word of praise does more good than pages of well-meant criticism.

LOVINGKINDNESS

For thy lovingkindness is before mine eyes, and I have walked in thy truth.

PSALM 26:3

Growing With God

*T*he loyalty you feel for your beloved is precious beyond words. Tell your mate you will "stand fast" all the way. It's easy to be gracious, when you're riding the crest of personal success. Be there for the hard times, too.

LOYALTY

And Ruth said, Entreat me not to leave thee, or to return from following after thee: for whither thou goest, I will go; and where thou lodgest, I will lodge: thy people shall be my people, and thy God my God.

RUTH 1:16

285

Growing With God

*L*augh joyously with your beloved.
Lift your eyes to the sky and praise God for
the light He has given to you in your love
life together. He directs you in plentiful
paths. Walk them with joy and gladness.

LAUGHTER

*Light is sown for the righteous, and gladness
for the upright in heart.*
PSALM 97:11

Growing With God

*S*peak your emotions freely. Your love will flourish as a result of the outpouring of your heart. The same is true in your relationship with God. He wants you to tell Him how you feel. Speak your mind. Share your heart. God will listen and comfort you in all your ways.

OPENNESS

I cried with my whole heart; hear me, O Lord: I will keep thy statutes.
PSALM 119:145

Growing With God

*S*eek to love your mate with all the
fruits of the Spirit. Let your relationship be
a model for all others to see — especially if
you have a child. If you lack any of the
fruits, ask of the One who gives abundantly
to all who seek. Our God is loving and
generous. Ask and you will receive.

FRUITS

*But the fruit of the Spirit is love, joy, peace,
longsuffering, gentleness, goodness, faith,
Meekness, temperance: against such
there is no law.*

GALATIANS 5:22,23

Growing With God

*Y*ou can't earn love. Love is a gift. You can't buy love. It's simply not for sale. And it's especially true for God's love. God has given us love because He has chosen to do so. No one has ever been good enough or rich enough to earn His love. So it is with your spouse. No one is ever good enough to receive love. We love *simply because we choose to love.* Unconditional love is the most powerful force on earth.

CHOICE

...He delivered me, because he delighted in me.
PSALM 18:19b

Growing With God

*I*f you have a love thought for your beloved, speak it now! There are no guarantees from day to day. Take the time today to express your love. Live today with your love as though this were the last.

REGRET

For all flesh is as grass, and all the glory of man as the flower of grass. The grass withereth, and the flower thereof falleth away: But the word of the Lord endureth for ever...

1 PETER 1:24,25a

Growing With God

*T*he Bible says we are all equally precious in the eyes of God. Put your beloved's concerns on an equal footing with your own. Search for the best in your spouse. In so doing, your love relationship will flourish. Enjoy the dream of staying in love— *forever.*

EQUALS

There is neither Jew nor Greek, there is neither bond nor free, there is neither male nor female: for ye are all one in Christ Jesus.

GALATIANS 3:28

Growing With God

*S*hare your deepest reflections with your beloved. Talk often of the things on your mind and your heart. The more you share, the closer you'll come to each other in love and understanding. Give the one you love the gift of yourself.

REFLECTIONS

How precious also are thy thoughts unto me, O God! How great is the sum of them!
PSALM 139:17

Growing With God

*C*onceit is a dangerous ingredient in a love relationship. You're walking on eggshells when you begin to feel you are the only one who knows or understands the situation. Chances are you'll soon find yourself alone with your store of knowledge. Always look at both sides of the issue.

It still takes "two to tango."

CONCEIT

Seest thou a man wise in his own conceit?
There is more hope of a fool than of him.
PROVERBS 26:12

Growing With God

*L*ove your spouse and ask God to make your love blossom into a tree that shades your life together with goodness and contentment. Do not count the cost of love, look only to the end result of your togetherness.

BLOSSOM

So Boaz took Ruth, and she was his wife: and when he went in unto her, the Lord gave her conception, and she bare a son.

RUTH 4:13

Growing With God

*P*ray for your love relationship with the confidence that God will give you the desires of your heart. God listens to the pleas and your deepest concerns. His ears are waiting to hear your inner desires. He cares about you and your beloved.

WAITING

For the eyes of the Lord are over the righteous, and His ears are open unto their prayers....
I PETER 3:12a

Growing With God

*T*he Bible says the harmony of your love life affects the working of your prayers. God does not respond to your supplications the same if you pray from one side of your mouth while fighting with your mate out of the other. Let your life together be one of harmony.

TOGETHERNESS

Likewise, ye husbands, dwell with them according to knowledge, giving honour unto the wife, as unto the weaker vessel, and as being heirs together of the grace of life; that your prayers be not hindered.

I PETER 3:7

Growing With God

*B*uild up your beloved in the faith of Our Lord Jesus Christ. Encourage your mate with prayer and the witness of what God has done in your own life. Together grow in the knowledge of Him, His love and His goodness.

BUILD

But ye, beloved, building up yourselves on your most holy faith, praying in the Holy Ghost, Keep yourselves in the love of God, looking for the mercy of our Lord Jesus Christ unto eternal life.

JUDE 20,21

Growing With God

*S*tudy the Scriptures. Meditate on God's Word. Read His promises together with your beloved and talk about what His divine counsel means in your every day life. The Bible is as fresh today as when it was first given to humankind. Let it be your guide in your own loving relationship with your spouse.

PURE

The words of the Lord are pure words, as silver tried in a furnace of earth, purified seven times.
PSALM 12:6

Growing With God

*T*he farmer is not allowed to have a harvest the day after planting. A good crop takes time, patience and tender, loving care. It's akin to your relationship with your spouse. God is working to draw you and your beloved closer together *and to Him.*

GROWTH

Verily, verily, I say unto you, Except a corn of wheat fall into the ground and die, it abideth alone: but if it die, it bringeth forth much fruit.
JOHN 12:24

Growing With God

*B*y your example of love and caring, love your unbelieving mate into a relationship with God. Intrigue your spouse with words consistent with your loving actions. Show your beloved what a difference God continues to make in your own life. Love your mate into embracing the Gospel.

WITNESSING

And after certain days, when Felix came with his wife Drusilla, which was a Jewess, he sent for Paul, and heard him concerning the faith in Christ.

ACTS 24:24

Growing With God

*C*elebrate every success with your mate. Lift your arms and give thanks. Embrace the peaks of joy and happiness. God is in all good things. Applaud your mate's achievements with enthusiasm. Join together in thanksgiving.

SUCCESS

Then David returned to bless his household. And Michal the daughter of Saul came out to meet David, and said, How glorious was the king of Israel today...
II SAMUEL 6:20a

Growing With God

*T*he beginnings of love are like a vapour. There may be times when it will seem easier to just let it blow away. But God puts His angels before you and desires to stop the vapour from disappearing. Ask Him to keep your love alive. He wants the best for the two of you as you continue to share your life living and loving together.

BEGINNINGS

And the angel of the Lord went further, and stood in a narrow place, where was no way to turn either to the right hand or to the left.
NUMBERS 22:26

Growing With God

*T*reat your love like a precious jewel. Gaze at the sparkling stone, but do not smash it to see how it's been created. Leave some room for mystery. Let your love be a constant unraveling of the good things between you.

JEWEL

And Delilah said unto Samson, Hitherto thou hast mocked me, and told me lies:...And it came to pass, when she pressed him daily with her words, and urged him, so that his soul was vexed unto death; That he told her all his heart...
JUDGES 16:13a,16,17a

Growing With God

$\mathcal{G}$od binds up the rejected. If your beloved turns from you, know that you will be comforted in the arms of our Heavenly Father. He grieves with those who grieve and He comforts all who turn to Him. Rejection is painful. But whatever does not kill you *makes you stronger.*

COMFORT

For the Lord hath called thee as a woman forsaken and grieved in spirit, and a wife of youth, when thou wast refused, saith thy God.

ISIAH 54:6

Growing With God

$\mathcal{G}$od will always welcome you with open arms. No request is too small or too big to bring to Him. Tell our gracious Lord all that is on your heart regarding the one you love. Learn to pray for that which is difficult. While praying, anticipate God doing the impossible.

ANTICIPATION

But Jesus turned him about, and when he saw her, he said, Daughter, be of good comfort; thy faith hath made thee whole. And the woman was made whole from that hour.

MATTHEW 9:22

Rejoicing in Abundance

$\mathcal{T}$he Lord of all the heavens and earth has blessed you with His love and care. He delights in pleasing you throughout your days and in helping you and your beloved grow to full stature.

GROWING

I will sing unto the Lord, because he hath dealt bountifully with me.
PSALM 13:6

Rejoicing in Abundance

*G*ive and it shall be given back to you,
pressed down and overflowing. An open
heart and a gentle, open hand are the best
insurances of a long and lasting
love affair with your mate.

OVERFLOWING

*The liberal soul shall be made fat: and he that
watereth shall be watered also himself.*
PROVERBS 11:25

Rejoicing in Abundance

*G*od rains down His anointing power on His people. If you or your spouse have any lack, go to the Father who knows your every need. He will open His great storehouse of blessings and shower you with His generous heart.

ANOINTING

Thou anointest my head with oil; My cup runneth over. Surely goodness and mercy shall follow me all the days of my life; And I will dwell in the house of the Lord forever.
PSALM 23:5b,6

Rejoicing in Abundance

A smile can warm the coldest heart. Think on good things and your smile will radiate a contentment that will draw others to you. Adding more smiles to your marriage inevitably adds more romance to your life.

SMILES

A merry heart doeth good like a medicine: but a broken spirit drieth the bones.
PROVERBS 17:22

Rejoicing in Abundance

*I*f you and your spouse were to count all the wondrous things God has done for you, you would soon be overwhelmed. He gave you life, sustenance and continues to share with you His all-abiding love. He also gave you a mind and a heart to appreciate all He has given.

GIFTS

Come and hear, all ye that fear God, and I will declare what he hath done for my soul.
PSALM 66:16

Rejoicing in Abundance

*G*et a grip on hope and hang on tight.
Hope is the rope that rescues us from
despair and lethargy. Hang on tight and
keep expecting God to work a
miracle in your life.

HANG ON

*But I will hope continually, and will
yet praise thee more and more.*
PSALM 71:14

Rejoicing in Abundance

*C*ompliments bring a sparkle to everyone's eyes. Be a person who looks for reasons to compliment your beloved. Notice the fabric of your spouse's personality and give all the encouragement and praise you can.

PRAISE

The light of the eyes rejoiceth the heart: and a good report maketh the bones fat.
PROVERBS 15:30

Rejoicing in Abundance

*G*od's hand flung the moon into space and set the sun in its orbit. He holds the stars in His power and moves the seas at His whim. Rejoice in the special love He has created for you and your beloved.

CREATION

The day is thine, the night also is thine: thou has prepared the light and the sun.

PSALM 74:16

Rejoicing in Abundance

*L*ove your mate with abandonment. Don't measure your love and weigh what you receive in return. Be a lover who gives yourself today with no thought for the hurts of the past or the problems of the future.

UNMEASURED

Give, and it shall be given unto you; good measure, pressed down, and shaken together, and running over, shall men give into your bosom...
LUKE 6:38a

Rejoicing in Abundance

*J*f you feel alone and insignificant, don't despair. God lifts up the humble and comforts those who are abandoned. Bring your heart to Him for healing and new hope.

ENDURANCE

I watch, and am as a sparrow alone upon the house top...But thou, O Lord, shalt endure for ever; and thy remembrance unto all generations.
PSALM 102:7,12

Rejoicing in Abundance

*G*od has put His loving hand on the
pulse of your life and He has given you
wondrous gifts. Thank Him for the gift of
love He has given to you through
your special mate.

FAVOUR

Whoso findeth a wife findeth a good thing,
and obtaineth favour of the Lord.
PROVERBS 18:22

Rejoicing in Abundance

*S*avour each day and drink of its sweetness. Treasure each moment of vibrant life the Lord has given to you. Don't wile your hours or your days away waiting for what will be. Enjoy what is. Do it now!

ENJOY!

This is the day which the Lord hath made;
we will rejoice and be glad in it.
PSALM 118:24

Rejoicing in Abundance

*G*od has spread His mantle of
protection over your family. He loves the
ones you love even more than you do.
Come to Him as a family and ask for the
grace you each need to live out your days.

GRACE

*The Lord shall increase you more and more,
you and your children.*
PSALM 115:14

Rejoicing in Abundance

*L*ift your arms to the sky and thank God for the sunshine He has given to you. Every ounce of energy you have has been given to you by Him. Rejoice in the abundance of health and wealth He has given you and your beloved.

PROSPER

Beloved, I wish above all things that thou mayest prosper and be in health, even as thy soul prospereth.
III JOHN 1:2

Rejoicing in Abundance

*Y*our words of love are a sweet nectar to your beloved. Pour love words on the heart of your mate until you are both satiated. Celebrate your love and be enormously happy together.

SATIATED

How sweet are thy words unto my taste! yea, sweeter than honey to my mouth!
PSALM 119:103

Rejoicing in Abundance

*G*od has woven threads of gold throughout your life. Don't hesitate to remind yourself and others of the good things God has done for you in the past. It gives you reason to hope. Explore the good of days gone by...enjoy your past heritage and share it with others.

TESTIMONIES

Thy testimonies have I taken as a heritage for ever; for they are the rejoicing of my heart.
PSALM 119:111

Rejoicing in Abundance

Crown your life with honour. Be careful that scandal doesn't rightfully attach to your name. Live your life honestly and you and your beloved will enjoy peace in all your dealings.

HONOR

But above all things, my brethren, swear not, neither by heaven, neither by the earth, neither by any other oath; but let your yea be yea; and your nay, nay; lest ye fall into condemnation.
JAMES 5:12

Rejoicing in Abundance

*P*our warm laughter over your life
with your beloved. Ask the Father who
delights in each of us to teach you to
delight in the ways of each other as
children delight in each
new day's discoveries.

DELIGHT

He brought me forth also into a large place:
he delivered me, because he delighted in me.
II SAMUEL 22:20

Rejoicing in Abundance

*L*ove is a great treasure hunt. Seek to discover the priceless and the special facets of your beloved's heart and soul. One way to discover the treasures of your spouse is to read God's Word together and meditate on His love.

PRICELESS

I rejoice at thy word, as one that findeth great spoil.
PSALM 119:162

Rejoicing in Abundance

*L*ove your mate with an active, emotional love. Hear the joys and the sadness of the one you love. Remind your beloved of your steadfast love during the challenging times of your life.

EMOTIONAL

Then said Elkanah her husband to her, Hannah, why weepest thou? and why eatest thou not? and why is thy heart grieved? am not I better to thee than ten sons?

I SAMUEL 1:8

Rejoicing in Abundance

*R*efresh yourself with the love you share with your heart's partner. Shape your love into the same kind of love God gives to each of you. May your affection be a shade tree during life's dry seasons.

REFRESH

...the Lord is thy shade upon thy right hand. The sun shall not smite thee by day, nor the moon by night.
PSALM 121:5b,6

Rejoicing in Abundance

*F*eel the texture of your beloved's spirit. Spend time together in prayer so you know the soul of your mate as well as you know your own. It takes time...but you will be richer as a result of your caring.

SOUL

And fear not them which kill the body, but are not able to kill the soul: but rather fear him which is able to destroy both soul and body in hell.
MATTHEW 10:28

Rejoicing in Abundance

$\mathcal{D}$evelop a thankful heart. Look for reasons to be thankful to God and to your mate. A thankful tongue will water your relationship until love will blossom beyond your greatest expectations.

THANKFUL

Let the heavens rejoice, and let the earth be glad; let the sea roar, and the fulness thereof.
PSALM 96:11

Rejoicing in Abundance

*O*ffer criticism cautiously. In any
relationship, there are two sides to every
issue. Examine your own actions before
you turn a critical eye to the actions of
your mate. Your task is to love, not
criticize. If you need to change your
perspective, start changing
today, not tomorrow.

PERSPECTIVE

*And why beholdest thou the mote that is in thy
brother's eye, but perceivest not the beam
that is in thine own eye?*
LUKE 6:41

Rejoicing in Abundance

*F*orgiveness can make the sun shine on a marriage in trouble. It will make love sprout and grow in ground that once seemed barren. Don't bear grudges against your beloved. Freely forgive.

FORGIVENESS

*For thou, Lord, art good, and ready to forgive;
and plenteous in mercy unto all them
that call upon thee.*

PSALM 86:5

Rejoicing in Abundance

The ongoing challenges of life can place heavy burdens on you and your mate. Learn to lift the weight together so the troubles do not crush either of you. Almost any burden, when shared equally, can be borne. Flex your muscles together. The load will be lighter.

TROUBLES

They helped every one his neighbour; and every one said to his brother, Be of good courage.
ISAIAH 41:6

Rejoicing in Abundance

$\mathcal{G}$ive praise unto God.
Hold hands with your beloved and stand
before the Almighty in gratitude for who He
is and what He has done in your own
private world. Keep your eyes focussed on
Him and He will give you
a peace beyond understanding.

GRATITUDE

I will praise thee, O Lord, with my whole heart;
I will shew forth all thy marvellous works.

PSALM 9:1

Rejoicing in Abundance

*L*oneliness is a dark place.
Emptiness seems to surround you. Then
your beloved enters. The love of your
spouse is a bright and glowing candle
that lights every corner of
your solitary aloneness.

BRIGHTNESS

*Who being the brightness of his glory, and the
express image of his person...sat down on the
right hand of the Majesty on high.*
HEBREWS 1:3

Rejoicing in Abundance

*L*ittle words, like "Please forgive" or "I care" will make a big difference in your marriage. Don't neglect the seemingly *little* words; they speak richly of your special love and attention.

LITTLE THINGS

A word fitly spoken is like apples of gold in pictures of silver.
PROVERBS 25:11

Building A Family

*I*f you yearn for children and have none of your own, come to God in prayer. God delights in giving you good things. Ask Him to bless you with a child to love and to cherish.

CHILDREN

He maketh the barren woman to keep house, and to be a joyful mother of children. Praise ye the Lord.
PSALM 113:9

Building A Family

*I*f you want your child to grow to be a God-fearing man or woman, then you and your mate need to show him what God-fearing people live like. There is no substitute for a loving example. Be that example of God's love today.

EXAMPLE

...Blessed is the man that feareth the Lord, that delighteth greatly in his commandments.
PSALM 112:1b

Building A Family

*I*t is important to teach your child the law and the love of God. Read the scriptures *together* as a family. Give your child the chance to ask questions about your own beliefs. Say in words *he can understand* what God has done in the life of you and your mate.

LAW

...Forsake not the law of thy mother: For they shall be an ornament of grace unto thy head, and chains about thy neck.

PROVERBS 1:8b,9

Building A Family

*D*iscipline is a difficult area for
many families. Discuss with your mate how
you both wish to deal with the various
areas of challenge in raising children. Then
be both firm and compassionate in your
daily discipline — always speaking
the truth in love.

DISCIPLINE

*For whom the Lord loveth he correcteth; even as
a father the son in whom he delighteth.*
PROVERBS 3:12

Building A Family

*H*ave hope as you nurture your child. The Bible says the early training will abide with him even when he is old. Make it a happy habit to talk with your child, at an early age, about God's love.

TRAINING

Train up a child in the way he should go: and when he is old, he will not depart from it.
PROVERBS 22:6

Building A Family

*F*aith is contagious. When you and your spouse speak of your faith and live it in your every day lives, your child will be influenced by its power. Show your child how to have faith today.

FAITH

When I call to remembrance the unfeigned faith that is in thee, which dwelt first in thy grandmother Lois, and thy mother Eunice; and I am persuaded that in thee also.

II TIMOTHY 1:5

Building A Family

*T*each your child to tell the truth. A respect for honesty will serve him well throughout his entire life. Be sure to speak the truth yourself in your dealings with others. Your child will see it and follow your example.

TRUTH

I have no greater joy than to hear that my children walk in truth.
III JOHN 1:4

Building A Family

*G*uide your child with gentleness and kindness. Show your child kindness from an early age and train him with a godly affection. Even when you must discipline, be sure your child knows he is loved *simply for who he is.*

GENTLENESS

But we were gentle among you, even as a nurse cherisheth her children.
1 THESSALONIANS 2:7

Building A Family

*T*each your child to obey you. Early lessons in respect for authority provide your child with a firm base for success in relationships with others. When you are affectionate with your child, it is easier for him to want to do what you say.

OBEDIENCE

Children, obey your parents in the Lord: for this is right.
EPHESIANS 6:1

Building A Family

*D*on't be so stern with your child that you cause him to be angry and rebellious. Make every human effort to be fair and just in your rules and expectations and always handle your discipline with love.

REBELLION

Fathers, provoke not your children to anger, lest they be discouraged.
COLOSSIANS 3:21

Building A Family

*W*hen you train your child well, you will bear pleasant fruit in later years. A wise and righteous child will bring joy to the hearts of yourself and your spouse. Encourage your child in the ways of wisdom.

WISDOM

The father of the righteous shall greatly rejoice: and he that begetteth a wise child shall have joy of him.
PROVERBS 23:24

Building A Family

*T*he soul of your child is a precious trust from the Lord. God wants each of His children to come to know Him. Teach your child of God's love and pray for his eternal salvation.

ETERNAL SOUL

Even so it is not the will of your Father which is in heaven, that one of these little ones should perish.

MATTHEW 18:14

Building A Family

*L*eave a legacy for your child. When you have children, you immediately begin to care more deeply about the care and feeding of the nation and our physical world. Talk with your spouse about what you two can do to help make our planet a better place for your child to live.

LEGACY

One generation shall praise thy works to another, and shall declare thy mighty acts.
PSALM 145:4

Building A Family

*D*on't underestimate your child. The
natural dependency and openness of a
child is so precious that Jesus said it was
*childlike people who made up His
kingdom.* Encourage your child to keep
the enthusiasm of his early days — so that
it may serve him well as he
grows into an adult.

ENTHUSIASM

*But Jesus said, Suffer little children, and forbid
them not, to come unto me: for of such is
the kingdom of heaven.*
MATTHEW 19:14

Building A Family

$\mathcal{G}$od has made a commitment to you, your spouse, and your child. If you follow Him, He will remember you and redeem you. Be a gentle guide to your whole family as you yourself follow His counsel today.

COVENANT

He hath remembered his covenant for ever, the word which he commanded to a thousand generations.
PSALM 105:8

Building A Family

*Y*our child is a heritage from the Lord. He has placed your child in your care to delight you and to challenge you to grow into the person He wants you to be.

HERITAGE

Lo, children are an heritage of the Lord: and the fruit of the womb is his reward.
PSALM 127:3

Building A Family

*Y*our child is a blessing from God. He's given him to you for your love and nurture. Show him the way of God's truth. Let your life and love point your child to the Lord.

INSTRUCTION

My son, hear the instruction of thy father,...
PROVERBS 1:8a

351

Building A Family

 $\mathcal{G}$ od is the champion of children. It is an honor to have Him give a child into your care and the care of your spouse. But He also stands with you as you struggle to raise your children.

STRUGGLES

And whosoever shall offend one of these little ones that believe in me, it is better for him that a millstone were hanged about his neck, and he were cast into the sea.

MARK 9:42